Published by "Heart (
22 Chapel Lane, B
Southport, Lancashire.

Tel: - 44 (0)1704 228 394
Email: - heartofoak@safe-mail.net

ISBN> 0-9549462-1-9

First UK Edition 2007.

Printed and bound by: - Lightning source. Lightning source UK LTD 6 Precedent Drive, Rooksley, Milton Keynes, Bedfordshire. MK13 8PR, UK

The scriptures in this book are all from either the King James Bible; or the New International Version. Copyright (c) 1973, 1978, and 1984, by International Bible Society, unless otherwise stated.

Cover picture: Celtic Cross Wales.

Introduction.

To understand the death of Jesus on that first Good Friday, we need to appreciate the words He spoke, as he endured crucifixion. The Old Testament prophesied his death, the Epistles explain his death, but the seven words spoken by Christ, from the cross, take us to the heart of Easter. Each sentence, spoken through searing pain, was for a specific purpose, and each word will help us understand the implications of His death. These are not the normal cries of a dying man; they are words spoken with care and precision; words for the disciples, words for his family, and words for the whole world. Here we do not only come to understand why Christ died, but we lift the veil on the mystery of death itself.

From a human point of view Christ's death was a legal travesty, promoted by jealousy and hatred. From God's perspective Christ was *"the Lamb of God slain before the foundation of the earth"*. How man's evil can fulfil God's will is a profound mystery. The death of Jesus teaches us that nothing is outside God's control, and that in spite of man's perversity, God's purposes will finally triumph.

At the crucifixion we see God revealed both in His weakness, and in His glory, for in the execution of "God the Son", death itself is taken into the heart of God, God through Christ experiences the reality of death, then with the resurrection, destroys its power. Paul writes, *'O death, where is thy sting? O grave, where is thy victory? Thanks be to God, which gives us the victory through our Lord Jesus Christ. 1 Cor 15:55-57*

"The Seven Last Words" may be read by individuals or used by churches as a lent course / Bible class. It provides a comprehensive resource, helping us understand and celebrate Easter. If this course is used as a basis for Sunday worship, it should be started on the first Sunday in Lent ending on the resurrection morning. However one week is left empty to allow the church to celebrate Mothering Sunday or Palm Sunday, independently of the course.

It includes:-

1. A daily reading section leading us through the life of Christ in chronological order as we progress towards Easter.

2. Sermon outlines at the beginning of each chapter giving a preaching resource for Easter. Each outline is based on the material in the chapters, and could form the basis for six Sunday services.

3. Each chapter is accompanied with full resources for Lent groups, including questions, prayers, memory verses and action points. Ideally each group member will have their own copy of the book.

4. There is a linked selection of appropriate hymns, songs,

& readings for Sunday and small group worship see p152.

5. Sunday resources: - There are themed Bible readings for each week which can be used for Sunday or in discussion groups. A chronology of Good Friday is included for the first week and a chronology of Easter Sunday for the last. There are also dramatic readings to accompany week 1 or 5 and 6. An optional visual activity for the Sunday service is included where a bare cross may be dressed with different symbols of the passion each week.

6. If the course is used as a Lenten preaching programme, there are six chapters rather than seven so that churches can celebrate either Mothering Sunday or Palm Sunday independently of this course and still conclude on Easter morning.

The six studies take us from Christ's first words upon the cross, *"Father forgive them,"* to the morning of the resurrection, for without the resurrection the cross is incomplete. Travel with me to that first Easer as we consider Jesus, the man who destroyed death and brought life and immortality to light. We begin by setting the four Gospel accounts in their historic order.

The Passion of our Lord Jesus Christ.

John 19:17-22. Carrying his own cross, he went out to the place of the Skull (which in Aramaic is called Golgotha). Here they crucified him, and with him two others-- one on each side and Jesus in the middle. Pilate had a notice prepared and fastened to the cross. It read: JESUS OF NAZARETH, THE KING OF THE JEWS. Many of the Jews read this sign, for the place where Jesus was crucified was near the city, and the sign was written in Aramaic, Latin and Greek. The chief priests of the Jews protested to Pilate, "Do not write 'The King of the Jews', but that this man claimed to be king of the Jews." Pilate answered, "What I have written, I have written."

Luke 23:33-34. When they came to the place called the Skull, there they crucified him, along with the criminals-- one on his right, the other on his left. Jesus said, **"Father, forgive them, for they do not know what they are doing."** Mark **15:25+:27-30.** It was the third hour when they crucified him. --- Those who passed by hurled insults at him, shaking their heads and saying, "So! You, who are going to destroy the temple and build it in three days, come down from the cross and save yourself!" **Matt 27:40** "if you are the Son of God!"

John 19:23-24. When the soldiers crucified Jesus, they took his clothes, dividing them into four shares, one for each of them, with the undergarment remaining. This garment was seamless, woven in one piece from top to bottom. "Let's not tear it," they said to one another. "Let's decide by lot who will get it." This happened that the scripture might be fulfilled which said, "They divided my garments among them and cast lots for my clothing." So this is what the soldiers did.

Matt 27:41 -44. In the same way the chief priests, the teachers of the law and the elders mocked him. "He saved others," they said, "but he can't save himself! He's the King of Israel! Let him come down now from the cross, and we will believe in him. He trusts in God. Let God rescue him now if he wants him, for he said, 'I am the Son of God.'" The robbers who were crucified with him also heaped insults on him.

Luke 23:36-37. The soldiers also came up and mocked him. They offered him wine vinegar and said, "If you are the king of the Jews, save yourself." **John 19:25-27.** Near the cross of Jesus stood his mother, his mother's sister, Mary the wife of Clopas, and Mary Magdalene. When Jesus saw his mother there, and the disciple whom he loved standing near by, he said to his mother, **"Dear woman, here is your son," and to the disciple, "Here is your mother."** From that time on, this disciple took her into his home.

Luke 23:39-43. One of the criminals who hung there hurled insults at him: "Aren't you the Christ? Save yourself and us!" But the other criminal rebuked him. "Don't you fear God," he said, "since you are under the same sentence? We are punished justly, for we are getting what our deeds deserve. But this man

6

has done nothing wrong." Then he said, "Jesus, remember me when you come into your kingdom." Jesus answered him, **"I tell you the truth, today you will be with me in paradise."**

Mark 15:33-35. At the sixth hour darkness came over the whole land until the ninth hour. And at the ninth hour Jesus cried out in a loud voice, "Eloi, Eloi, lama sabachthani?"-- Which means, **"My God, my God, why have you forsaken me?"** When some of those standing near heard this, they said, "Listen, he's calling Elijah."

John 19:28-29. - knowing that all was now completed, and so that the Scripture would be fulfilled, Jesus said, **"I am thirsty."** A jar of wine vinegar was there; **Matt 27:48-19,** immediately one of them ran and got a sponge. He filled it with wine vinegar, put it on a stick, and offered it to Jesus to drink. The rest said, "Now leave him alone. Let's see if Elijah comes to save him." **John 19:30.** When he had received the drink, Jesus said, **"It is finished."** **Luke 23:46** (and) called out with a loud voice, **"Father, into your hands I commit my spirit.** When he had said this, he breathed his last. **John 19:30.** With that, he bowed his head and gave up his spirit.

Matt 27:51-53. At that moment the curtain of the temple was torn in two from top to bottom. The earth shook and the rocks split. **Mark 15:39.** When the centurion, who stood there in front of Jesus, heard his cry and saw how he died, he said, "Surely this man was the Son of God!"

Index.

Death & Glory

Luke 23:26-38.

Father Forgive them they do not know what they are doing. v34.

The Open Door. (Rev 4:1, John 10:9)

What do these words teach us?

1. Our need for forgiveness.

2. Whose forgiveness we need.

3. Who paid for our forgiveness? (Heb 5:9, 9:22)

Who were THEY? (Three representative groups.)

1. The Ordinary people.

They Misunderstood. (Mk 15:29-30, John 2:18-21.)

They Doubted. *"If you are the Son of God."* (Mt 27:39-40, John 5:18 + 10:31-33)

2. The Rulers. (Chief Priests, Teachers and Elders.)

They Stubbornly Resisted his Kingship. (John 19:19-21, John 18:37 also Mt 27:41f, John 10:18, Mt 26:53.)

3. The Soldiers. They were not interested in Jesus. (Mt 27:30 Psalm 22, Mk 15:39.)

The same old excuses. *"They do not know what they are doing."*

Excusing ignorance, or greater forgiveness?

How should we respond? (John 8:11, 1Tim 1:13, Acts 3:15+17f.)

1: Death and Glory.

(Luke 23:26-38)

'Father Forgive them they do not know what they are doing'. v34.

Jesus spoke seven times from the cross. To find each saying and place them in order we must search the four gospels. The first is recorded in Luke and is Christ's prayer of forgiveness. *"When they came to the place called the Skull, there they crucified him, along with the criminals-one on his right, the other on his left. Jesus said, "Father, forgive them, for they do not know what they are doing." Luke 23:3-34.*

This first cry from the cross speaks of both DEATH & GLORY. The idea is familiar to anyone who knows the events of June 6th 1944. On that day the allied armies commenced the D-day landings in Normandy. On the first day, 57,000 US troops and 75,000 British and Canadian troops were landed. Five beach heads were established and soon the allies were pouring back into Europe, to liberate her from Nazi occupation. On the same day 2,500 allied troops died and 8,500 were wounded. I have several friends who served in this operation, some went ahead as Paratroopers to take key installations, others followed days later, (D day + 5 etc) continuing the battle. Europe was potentially liberated that day, but it took over a year for the war to finally end. The door was opened, the victory was unstoppable, but there were still battles to be won before peace was finally achieved.

Jesus' death opened a far greater door than D-Day; it opened the very door of heaven itself. His death meant our liberation. The apostle John writes, *"After this I looked, and there before me was a door standing open in heaven." (Rev 4:1)* Jesus said, *"I am the door. If anyone enters by Me, he will be saved." (John 10:9)* NKJV

The Victory was instantaneous, freedom from sin and death were proclaimed for all, but there are still battles to be fought before the final peace is established. Each time a person submits their will and places their faith in Jesus, the battle is won on their behalf. The Cross has liberated us, the question is do we know we have been liberated?

I remember the story of an old Circus bear; when its performing days were over, it was retired to a Safari Park. The problem was that for many years the bear had been kept in a cage, where it could only walk ten paces in one direction, then turn and take ten paces back in the other direction. The day of the release came, the bear and its cage were transported to the park, the door was opened, and the keeper retreated quickly. The bear walked towards the open door, stopped, turned round and walked back, ten paces in the other direction. It never left the cage. Next the bear was sedated and the cage was dismantled. When the bear woke, it was free. It stood, shook itself, walked ten paces in one direction, then turned and walked back ten paces in the other direction. Though there were no bars, they were still there in its mind. The keeper had no choice but to destroy the bear. The habits of a lifetime, kept it from finding freedom. The last words of Jesus proclaim our freedom, but we must begin to live in that freedom liberated from the habits and sins which cage us. Receiving His forgiveness is the first step, following Him is the second.

This is the heart of the Christian faith, the substitutionary atoning death of Christ. (He died in my place, to cover my sins, and so turn away God's judgement form my head.) Here is our doorway to heaven and our boast on earth (Gal 6:4). No Christian can ever claim that they deserve a place in heaven, they can never boast in their achievements, but must boast in what Jesus has done. Paul writes, *"no-one may boast before him."* -Then he adds, *"Let him who boasts boast in the Lord"* *1Cor 1:29 + 31*. The door to "the Glory" is open, and we glory in the one who opened it.

What do these words teach us?
They tell us of **our need, the father's mercy, and Christ's mediation**. In Christ's first cry we see 1: Our need of

forgiveness. (Forgive them) 2: Who we are to ask for forgiveness (Father). 3: Who purchased our forgiveness, (Jesus). Here, Christ is a mediator, offering His High Priestly prayer on our behalf. *"Father forgive them"* is His cry, *"They do not know what they are doing."*

Jesus as mediator of the New Covenant is asking forgiveness from an offended God. He is not simply praying for His executioners, but for all who are ignorant of their sin and need of forgiveness. He is acting as our great High Priest, bringing His request before the Father, including all people through all time in His prayer. The ministry of the High Priest is described in *Heb 5:1 "Every high priest is selected from among men and is appointed to represent them in matters related to God, to offer gifts and sacrifices for sins".* The High Priest in the Temple could never enter the presence of God without sacrificial blood. It was the blood which granted admission to God's presence and bought forgiveness. *"In fact, the law requires that nearly everything be cleansed with blood and without the shedding of blood there is no forgiveness" (Heb 9:22).* Jesus, as both Priest and Sacrifice, offers up His own blood on the cross, for all of our sins.

The timing of Christ's first cry is important. It came as Jesus was being nailed to the cross. *"When they came to the place called the Skull, there they crucified him, along with the criminals-- one on his right, the other on his left. Jesus said, "Father, forgive them, for they do not know what they are doing." Luke 23:33-34 NIV.* The very moment they began to crucify Him, He prayed, *"Father forgive them."*

The first Bishop of Liverpool J.C. Ryle wrote: "As soon as the blood of the great sacrifice began to flow, the great High Priest began to intercede". This is Christ's High Priestly prayer, offering His blood as the one eternal sacrifice for sin. With this prayer the door of heaven is opened.

We have already touched on the universal nature of Christ's sacrifice, but who is Jesus specifically praying for? When He prays *"Father forgive **Them,**"* who are "They"?

Three Groups were involved in the crucifixion: the ordinary people, the Chief Priests or rulers, and the Romans.

The ordinary people are mentioned in *Mark 15:29-3:, **Those who passed by** hurled insults at him, shaking their heads and saying, "So! You, who are going to destroy the temple and build it in three days, come down from the cross and save yourself!"* These are not the rulers or Romans, they are ordinary people. The same people probably heard His sermon on the mount, perhaps some are led by the angry crowd; but why did they insult Him?

1, It seems that they felt that Jesus had let them down. They remembered His promise, to rebuild the Temple in three days and saw He couldn't even save Himself. This promise was given three years earlier, at the beginning of His ministry, when Jesus cleansed the Temple; they thought it was an empty boast. The Jews had challenged Him, *"What miraculous sign can you show us to prove your authority to do all this?"* Jesus answered them, *"Destroy this temple, and I will raise it again in three days." The Jews replied, "It has taken forty-six years to build this temple, and you are going to raise it in three days?" But the temple he had spoken of was his body. After he was raised from the dead, his disciples recalled what he had said. Then they believed the Scripture and the words that Jesus had spoken. John 2:18-22.* After the resurrection John understood that Jesus meant the temple of His body, but as He died the people misunderstood and branded Him a liar. In three short days He would fulfil His promise.

2, The crowds were also sceptical of His claim to be God's Son. *"Those who passed by hurled insults at him, shaking their heads and saying, --- Come down from the cross, **if you are the Son of God**!" Matt 27:39-40.* They knew His claim to be the Son of God, but had no faith in Him. Calling Jesus *"The Son of God;"* means accepting that He is no less than God Himself. My sons are no less significant than I am, though younger, they are by nature fully human. This seems obvious, but people often miss the point. When a man has a son it must be a man. It is a law of nature that each species begets according to its own kind. A swan lays an egg which hatches into a cygnet, and grows to be a swan. A horse has a foal which becomes a horse, a cat has kittens and a woman has a human child. This means that if God is to beget a child, and that is what the Scriptures say (Jn1:18, John 3:16 + 18. Acts 13:33, Heb 1:5, 5:5, 11:17. 1Jn 4:9.), then His Son must be of the same nature as the father. If God begets a Son, that Son must posses the very nature of God Himself. The Son of God is no less than God Himself.

The Jews understood that by calling himself God's Son, Jesus was claiming to be equal with God. *John 5:18 "Therefore the Jews sought all the more to kill Him, because He not only broke the Sabbath, but also said that God was His Father, making Himself equal with God" NKJV.* The people understood his claims, but their faith could not rise to accept that this man was God in the flesh. This means when they rejected the Son, they were really rejecting God Himself.

It is the heart of the Christian faith, to see in Christ the very essence of God living among men. The Nicene Creed is the classical formula. "We believe in one Lord Jesus Christ, the only Son of God, eternally begotten of the father, God from God, Light from Light, true God from true God, begotten not made, of one being with the father." This was a constant difficulty for the Jews; they understood Christ's claims but did not believe Him. How could this man now standing before them be one with the God of all creation? Their mind could not accept such a possibility, so they rejected the author of life. *John 10:31-33 "Again the Jews picked up stones to stone him, but Jesus said to them, "I have shown you many great miracles from the Father. For which of these do you stone me?" "We are not stoning you for any of these," replied the Jews, "but for blasphemy, because you, a mere man, claim to be God."*

The people turned from Jesus because they misunderstood his words, they felt let down and did not accept him as the Son of God. Surely if he was the Son of God, he would be saved the agony of crucifixion? To the Sceptical crowd the cross was a test, and when Jesus died they felt sure that he had failed the test!

The next group are the chief priests, teachers and elders. They represent the politically powerful, the educated, wealthy and religious classes. If the ordinary people misunderstood Jesus, the rulers chose not to believe. Their vested interests kept them from faith!

Why was Jesus actually crucified? The usual way to find out the crime was to read the charge placed above the criminal. For Jesus the charge read, *JESUS OF NAZARETH, THE KING OF*

THE JEWS. Pilate himself wrote it, *"in Aramaic, Latin and Greek." John 19:19.* The chief Priest complained about the charge, *"Do not write 'The King of the Jews, but that this man claimed to be king of the Jews." (John 19:21)* If we go back to the genealogy of Jesus in Luke's Gospel, we will see he was a direct descendent of David's kingly line. He actually had the right to be king by birth. Pilate knew nothing of this but recognised his kingly bearing. *"Pilate therefore said to Him, "Are You a king then?" Jesus answered, "You say rightly that I am a king. For this cause I was born and for this cause I have come into the world, that I should bear witness to the truth. Everyone who is of the truth hears My voice" John 18:37 NKJV.* Pilate was not to be deterred, when the High Priest complained, he responded, *"what I have written, I have written." John 19:22.* King Jesus was something the leaders would not accept.

The thought of a suffering king was incomprehensible to the leaders. To kill Jesus would stop him becoming king, yet Jesus Said, *"My Kingdom is not of this world."* Save yourself, if you are the King *"and we will believe"* called the priests." Mt 27:43. What they could not know was that in saving others, he himself had to die. They called for a miracle of deliverance; they said "seeing is believing!" Theirs was an empty boast, when Jesus returned from the grave three days later, they still refused to believe. Stubbornness is the essence of unbelief; many people demand proof and then explain away the answer they receive.

God does not have to prove himself to a stubborn world. He has already proved his love in Christ's death and his power through the resurrection. Those who claim, they will "believe it when they see it", are just like these priests in Jerusalem, even a miracle won't convince them.

The rulers saw an impotent Christ, someone who was defeated and could not save himself. The idea that his death was saving others never entered their minds. The Bible is clear Jesus could have saved himself, but chose not to so that he could offer himself as a sacrifice for our sin upon the cross. (John 10:18, Mt 26:53)

The Soldiers were the next group of bystanders. They had no interest in Jesus; they mocked him with malice & brutality. *"They spat on him, and took the staff and struck him on the head again and again." Matthew 27:30.* He was not their king; he was a criminal from a conquered race. Their brutality and hatred of Jesus was vicious. Yet even their actions were foreseen. Psalm 22 described in detail the crucifixion over 1000 years before it happened.

"All who see me mock me; they hurl insults, shaking their heads: "He trusts in the LORD; let the LORD rescue him. Let him deliver him, since he delights in him." "I am poured out like water, and all my bones are out of joint. My heart has

turned to wax; it has melted away within me. I can count all my bones; people stare and gloat over me. They divide my garments among them and cast lots for my clothing". The end of the Psalm shows the purpose behind the crucifixion, *"All the ends of the earth will remember and turn to the LORD, and all the families of the nations will bow down before him." (Ps 22:27)*

To the Romans Jesus was nobody; only the lowest of criminals were crucified. To God this was the most important moment in the whole of human history; the Lamb of God was bearing the sins of the world. From now on the ends of the earth could turn to the Lord, and all the families of nations would bow down before him. The door to heaven is opened, but the minds of the executioners are closed. Then at the moment of His death the Centurion in command realises who Christ is. *Mark 15:39 "when the centurion, who stood there in front of Jesus, heard his cry and saw how he died, he said, "Surely this man was the Son of God!"*

We still make the same old excuses.

These three groups of people surrounding the cross represent people's attitudes today. People still feel let down by God; they have no real faith yet ask God to prove himself. "I will believe it when I see it," is the cry of the sceptic. When something goes wrong, they feel that God has let them down. It may be a marriage problem, or difficulties at work. It may be that someone they love is suffering, or they have ill health themselves. The point is that trials can either turn us to God, in dependence and faith, or away from him in scepticism. We can be like Job, *"Though He slay me, yet will I trust Him"* or we can be like the disappointed crowds, "**IF** you are the son of God do something". God does not need to prove his love to us; the cross was the ultimate demonstration of his love. He accepted Judgement as a sinner, and we were declared free. The problem is not that God does not act; the problem is, just like the crowds, we do not understand what he has done. We still do not expect a Messiah who suffers.

The rulers were **stubborn unbelievers.** They would not accept Christ as King; it would affect their position and life style. They led the way in asking for proof, but when it came they refused to believe, even inventing excuses to cover their own lack of faith. Matt 28:12-15 *"When the chief priests had met with the elders and devised a plan, they gave the soldiers a large sum of money, telling them, "You are to say, 'His disciples came during the night and stole him away while we were asleep.' If this report gets to the governor, we will satisfy him and keep you out of trouble."* Those who do not want to believe will always find an excuse, even when the truth is right in front of them. Stubborn unbelief has not changed.

The Roman Soldiers represent the **disinterested person**. They were the masters and Jesus was nothing to them, but their brutality and hatred still flowed out in beatings and mockery. It is revealing how someone who says they are not interested in Jesus can be so violent against him! They thought they were just obeying orders, he also prayed for their forgiveness. If we find we are fighting against the claims of Christ, we are not disinterested; we are in fact opposing Him. It was their sin which drove the nails into his hands, and his blood flowed for their forgiveness. If we feel this Jesus has nothing to do with us, he prays for us *"father forgive them."* At the Cross we either mock Christ or we confess Him as King, we can not be a casual bystander.

"They do not know what they are doing."

As Jesus prays for his executioners, he knows that they do not understand. He not only prays, *Father, forgive* them, he also pleads; *"for they do not know what they are doing."* He is not making excuses for sin. He is not saying forgive them, <u>because</u> of their ignorance. What Jesus is saying, is forgive even this ignorant sin, forgive this lack of understanding. They are ignorant, angry and perverse, they have no excuse, Father forgive even this. In Law we understand that ignorance is no excuse. Not knowing we have broken a law, will not keep us from prosecution. It is a great sin to ignore Jesus, and misunderstanding the cross will never bring us forgiveness. But when we come to see why Christ died, and believe he died for us, then our ignorance will be forgiven, and we will be accepted, even though we did not know what we were doing.

Jesus asks God to forgive their hard hearts, blind eyes and ignorant hatred. This is not an excuse for sin; it is a plea for greater forgiveness. There is hope for us here, we have not always understood Christ's death, some of us have mocked, and others ignored him, Christ prays for us too.

How should we respond? In the same way believers have always responded. Jesus said to the woman caught in adultery, *"neither do I condemn you,"* -- *"Go now and leave your life of sin."* John 8:11 Paul says, *"Even though I was once a blasphemer and a persecutor and a violent man, I was shown mercy because I acted in ignorance and unbelief."* 1 Tim 1:13. Once Paul recognised his ignorance, he turned to follow Christ. Peter addressed the crowd on the day of Pentecost, only 50 days after the Crucifixion. Many who witnessed Christ's death were present, *"You killed the author of life, but God raised him from the dead. -- Now, brothers, I know that you acted in ignorance, as did your leaders. But this is how God fulfilled what he had foretold through all the prophets, saying that his Christ would suffer. Repent, then, and turn to God, so that your sins may be wiped out, that times of refreshing may come from the Lord,"* Acts 3:15 + 17-20

Ignorance was no excuse, the answer is to turn in repentance to God and prove our repentance by following his Son. God is willing to forgive. Christ is still our high priest today; He offers his prayer and his blood for our forgiveness. If we are ignorant of his sacrifice, we must turn to him, and echo the prayer of Jesus, *"Father, forgive me I did not know what I was doing."*

Week one! Study Questions.

- Group reading: "The passion account" p5.
- Related reading: Isaiah 53:1-12. How many references to the cross does Isaiah have?
- Suggested songs and Hymns are in the Appendices p150.
- Questions marked with an* are key questions on the passage.

Groups do not need to cover all the questions.

A: Which part of Chapter One specially spoke to you?

B: Christ as High priest.

1: Why is the timing of this first cry important?

2*: What does it mean that Christ won a victory over sin, death and Hell at the cross? (Col 2:15; 1Cor 15:55-57)

2b: In what way is the victory complete and in what way is the battle still being fought?

3: Why do Christians pray in the name of Jesus?   1Tim 2:5.

C: Our response.

4: How is your Christian life complete yet incomplete?   Rom 8:22-23.

5: Do Christians acknowledge or hide their sins? (Who from?)

6*: What excuses might people make for sin in their lives?

D: The people, the Priests, the Romans.

7: In what way do people still misunderstand Jesus claims?

8*: Have you ever felt let down by God? Is it because you expected Him to do something He did not promise to do?

9: Have you met someone stubbornly unwilling to accept an answer?

10: Do riches and power tend to keep people from God and why?

11: Are we forgiven because of our ignorance, or did Jesus say even ignorance is forgivable?

12: How should we respond to this prayer of Christ?

A Prayer.

Father forgive, when counting this world too dear, we forsake your Son and forget your love.

Forgive us Lord when in pride we say: "I have no sins to confess today."

Forgive us when in scoffing rude, our lives and words betray your blood. Spirit of God, come cleanse us now and by your power apply the blood. Our High Priest stands in heaven above, His prayer is sure, His hands drip love.

Thank you Lord Jesus that today you still stand as High Priest praying for all who come in faith to you. Thank you that we may draw near to the Father through the sacrifice of the Son in the power of the Holy Spirit Amen.

Memory verse Week 1: - *"At present we do not see everything subject to him. But we see Jesus, who was made a little lower than the angels, now crowned with glory and honour because he suffered death, so that by the grace of God he might taste death for everyone." Heb 2:8-9*

Action point: -

- Is there anyone I need to forgive?
- Is there anyone I need to ask to forgive me?
- Pray first and then go and seek forgiveness!

Activity for the whole Church:-

- During the Sunday service erect a bare wooden cross at the front of the church. This will remind us of our focus in the weeks ahead. If possible the cross should be head height and could be made form the branches of last years Christmas tree, thus linking the birth of Christ with the death of Christ. Each week articles will be added to the cross.

- Verse to be read before the cross. *Isaiah 53:4-5 'Surely he has borne our grief, and carried our sorrows: yet we esteemed him stricken, smitten of God, and afflicted. He was wounded for our transgressions; he was bruised for our iniquities: the chastisement of our peace was laid upon him; and with his stripes we are healed. KJV*

A New Family, a New Faith!

"Dear woman, here is your son," and to the disciple,
"Here is your mother." John 19:27

A new Family for Mary. (John 19:25-27.)

A practical gesture.

- The fulfilment of Prophecy. LK 2:34-35.
- Preserving the Birth Narrative.

A Symbolic gesture. Matthew 16:18.

- What is a Church? Acts 2:42.
- The 'ekklasia.' Acts 19:39.
- Who do you say I am? Mt 16:13-18.
- The Family of Believers. Acts 2:36, Col 1:18.

A Growing Faith. Mk 3:31-35,

- Trusting MY Saviour. Luke 1:46-47.
- The natural family & the spiritual family.
- With the 120. Acts 1:13-14.
- Filled with the Holy Spirit. Acts 2:1-4, John 13:34.

2: A New Family, a new Faith!

John 19:25-27. "Near the cross of Jesus stood his mother, his mother's sister, Mary the wife of Clopas, and Mary Magdalene. When Jesus saw his mother there, and the disciple whom he loved standing nearby, he said to his mother, "Dear woman, here is your son," and to the disciple, "Here is your mother." From that time on, this disciple took her into his home."

A new Family for Mary. (John 19:25-27.)

In these verses we stand under the shadow of the cross. When Christ first spoke on the cross as both High Priest & sacrifice, he was praying for our forgiveness and offering his blood for the sins of the world. Now he turns to his friends and family standing in torment under the shadow of the cross. All the disciples except John have deserted him, four women remain, four soldiers gamble for his clothes, and the curious crowd drinks in the spectacle. As the women weep, Jesus through the pain of crucifixion speaks to John and to Mary.

This is the fulfilment of the prophecy she received at the temple in Jerusalem eight days after Christ's birth. *Luke 2:34-35 "Simeon blessed them and said to Mary, his mother: "This child is destined to cause the falling and rising of many in Israel, and to be a sign that will be spoken against, so that the thoughts of many hearts will be revealed. And a sword will pierce your own soul too."* With his second cry Jesus brought Mary into the family of God's Church.

It was a practical gesture.

Joseph is dead; Jesus the eldest son is about to die and Mary will be without care or support. The life of a widow was difficult in Israel, so Jesus turns to John *"the beloved disciple"* and gives the care of Mary into his hands. John would care for Mary & Mary would prove a source of inspiration, to John and the other disciples. She alone knew the story of the miraculous conception, the virgin birth, and early life of Jesus. With a word Jesus preserves his mother and the amazing story she alone carries of the virgin birth, the ride to Bethlehem, the prophecy in Jerusalem and the flight to Egypt. These secrets are kept for the Gospel writers to later record. The scripture tells us that John took this task seriously for *"From that time on, this disciple took her into his home."*

It was a symbolic gesture.

Mary and John were distant relatives but had little in common. She was a widow from the hill country of Nazareth, he a fisherman from Galilee. What brought them together at the cross was their love for Jesus, and it was this love of Christ that the new Christian family was to be based on. A family based on different ties than blood, a family bound together by faith in the

Crucified one. They shared an experience and they shared a faith. It is this faith in the crucified one which was the foundation stone of the Church.

It is the same message Jesus had entrusted to Peter when he said, *"On this rock I will build My church, and the gates of Hades shall not prevail against it."* *Matt 16:18 NKJV*

When Jesus said, "I will build My Church," what did he have in mind? What is the Church? I know of a man who never attended worship, but as he grew older he would sometimes go and sit in the Church building. If you asked him where he had been, he would certainly say that he had been to Church. In my home town, the Parish Church of St Oswald's is a tourist attraction. It has a beautifully carved vaulted ceiling and as Malpas was a royalist area, in the civil war, Cromwell stabled his horses there as an act of defiance. Does the presence of horses defile a church?

To some the Church is the building; in some areas of Wales you can direct people by Churches more easily than pubs. To others it is the heart of parish life, an institution which is part of the fabric of society; it stands for traditional values and cares for people in times of need. Over the last century the Church became increasingly associated with the great events of family life, it was there at birth, at marriage & death. This has been called the hatch, match & dispatch religion. This religion is now loosing its appeal; and is this the real purpose of the Church?

Our Church background will to a great extent affect the way we look at what Church is. If we have no connection with a church community we will think of it as an old building for old people, perhaps narrow minded people with little relevance to our lives today. If we come from a Roman Catholic background, we may well see the Church as the one institution ordained by God to carry the authority of Christ on earth. A Congregationalist may tend to sees the Church in purely local terms as the individual expression of the body of Christ in the local area. The Pentecostal or Charismatic would see the church as the realm where the Holy Spirit rules today.

With so many differing ideas about the Church how do we know what Christ had in mind when he said *"I will build my Church?"*

The only answer is to go to the Bible and measure our ideas of Church against the original vision of Jesus. Here we come across a problem. The word Church does not actually appear in the Bible. If we go to the Vines Dictionary of New testament words we will find that he word which we translate as Church is "ekklasia", and its correct translation would be congregation or assembly. Some languages don't even try to translate the word they simply transliterate the letters, so in Welsh the word for

Church is "Eglwys", in French it is "église".

The Greek word is actually two words put together, the first "ek" means "out of", the second "klesis" means "to call" or "a calling". So when Jesus said: "I will build my Church", he was saying: "I will call out my followers and join them together as a body of people, committed both to me and to each other". This is Church and it is demonstrated in the Acts of the Apostles. Those who accepted the message Peter preached on the first Pentecost, "continued steadfastly in the apostles' doctrine and fellowship, and in breaking of bread, and in prayers." Acts 2:42 KJV

There is one further word which may help us, the related word; kaleo was used of a group of people who were appointed to discuss important affairs. (Acts 19:39) So the Church is a group of people who have been called out, to gather together a round a vitally important purpose. They are called by Christ, out of the world, into the Kingdom of God and into fellowship with each other as a family of believers. They are an alternative community and that community is established on the call and confession of Jesus Christ.

What makes a group of believers a Church rather than a friendly club, a sports club, or social institute? It is the shared confession of Jesus Christ as Lord, and this is the confession

Peter made at Caesarea.

The disciples are in the region of Mt. Hermon (Caesarea Philippi) they are near the head waters of the Jordan, and as far as they can get from Jerusalem without leaving Israel. Jesus is about to begin His long walk back to crucifixion. Caesarea was a pagan city and pagan gods were worshipped on this very hillside. Amid this idolatry Jesus turns to his disciples and a moment of decision is reached. Matt 16:13-18 *"When Jesus came to the coasts of Caesarea Philippi, he asked his disciples, 'Who do men say that I the Son of man am?' And they said, some say John the Baptist: some, Elijah; and others, Jeremiah, or one of the prophets. But who do you say that I am? [He asked] And Simon Peter answered, 'Thou art the Christ, the Son of the living God.' Jesus said to him, Blessed art thou, Simon Bar-Jonas: for flesh and blood has not revealed it to you, but my Father which is in heaven; And I say to you, that you at Peter, and upon this rock I will build my church; and the gates of hell shall not prevail against it."* (KJV modernized.)

This confession of Jesus as the Christ, the son of the living God is the rock on which the Church is established. The true church consists of all who confess the name of Jesus. It is the body of believers who claim Him as Lord. Peter's first sermon put this very claim before the crowds on Pentecost morning, he said, *"let* all the house of Israel know assuredly that God has made this Jesus, whom you crucified, both Lord and Christ." Acts 2:36. NKJV. The earliest creed of the Christian faith is found in Phil 2:11 and it reads "Jesus Christ is Lord, to the glory of God the Father".

This is the church those who have been called by Jesus and are now joined as a body of believers. We may come to chapel but we are not part of the Church until we confess the lordship of Christ in our lives. This is the foundation stone, without it the building collapses. A solitary Christian is a contradiction, we are united by faith to him who "is the head of the body, the church;" Col 1:18.

We stand on the confession of the Lordship of Christ, which makes nonsense of the saying "you don't have to go to Church to be a Christian." If we claim to be Christian but are not connected to the family of faith, we are not following the pattern of Jesus. He said "I will build my Church and the gates of Hell will not prevail". (Matthew 16:18) When anyone places their faith in Christ they are part of this new the church family and related through his blood, to all who love Christ. Many people believe in God, but Christians are called to be part of his family the Church. It is the love of Christ that unites us and the blood of Christ which cleanses us. By bringing Mary under the care of the Apostle John – the Apostle who would live the longest – she is at the very centre of Christ's new community the church.

A Growing Faith. Mk 3:31-35, Acts 1:13-14.

As Mary sang her prophetic song the Magnificat, *"My soul glorifies the Lord and my spirit rejoices in God my Saviour;"* *Luke 1:46-47* She could have had little conception of what it meant to be mother of the saviour. She begins her journey with great faith and obedience, but we are told "Mary kept all these things, and pondered them in her heart" Luke 2:19 KJV. It was only after the cross that full understanding came.

Mary did not always grasp that Jesus mission was to give His life as a sacrifice for sin, and by doing so; to establish a new family of faith. Many theologians believe that in Jesus' early ministry she came with her other children to remonstrate with him, His natural family trying to curb his spiritual zeal. *Mark 3:31-35: Then Jesus' mother and brothers arrived. Standing outside, they sent someone in to call him. A crowd was sitting around him, and they told him, "Your mother and brothers are outside looking for you." "Who are my mother and my brothers?" he asked. Then he looked at those seated in a circle around him and said, "Here are my mother and my brothers! Whoever does God's will is my brother and sister and mother."*

Jesus priority was establishing the family of God. At the time Mary did not understand, but now at the cross Jesus places her

36

under care of the Apostle John, at the very heart of this new family of faith. In Acts chapter one, we find her devoted to prayer and waiting with the 120 disciples for the promised Holy Spirit. *"When they arrived, they went upstairs to the room where they were staying. Those present were Peter, John, James and Andrew; Philip and Thomas, Bartholomew and Matthew; James son of Alphaeus and Simon the Zealot, and Judas son of James. They all joined together constantly in prayer, along with the women and **Mary the mother of Jesus, and with his brothers.**" Acts 1:13-14.* Her family had become part of the larger family of faith, and when the Holy Spirit filled the Apostles on the day of Pentecost; Mary was one who saw the tongues of fire, heard the wind of the Spirit and spoke in tongues as the Spirit enabled her. *"And when the day of Pentecost was fully come, they were all with one accord in one place. And suddenly there came a sound from heaven as of a rushing mighty wind, and it filled the entire house where they were sitting. And there appeared to them cloven tongues like as of fire, which rested upon each of them. And they were all filled with the Holy Ghost, and began to speak with other tongues, as the Spirit gave them utterance" Acts 2:1-4.*

The Church is truly more than an organisation, it is the realm where the Spirit of God rules, it is the place where "His Kingdom should come and His will be done, on earth as in heaven." When Jesus calls us, he does not simply call us **to**

believe, he calls us **to belong** to his Church, he calls us not just to love God but to be filled with his Spirit and to love each other. (See Mark 12:30-31.)

At the last supper Jesus gave a last commandment, *"A new commandment I give to you, that you love one another; as I have loved you, - By this all will know that you are My disciples, if you have love for one another" John 13:34 NKJV.* In His death Jesus brought Mary into the Church and prepared her for the coming of the Holy Spirit. This is still his plan today, to bring all believers into God's new family Church and fill them with His Holy Spirit. Mary and John shared a faith, a family and an experience, so do God's people today, the cross the family, and the Spirit, are the marks of the true church, for the Church is the realm where the Holy Spirit rules, and where true family love is shared.

Week Two: Study Questions.

- Suggested Hymns and songs are in the appendices p150.
- Group reading John 19:16-30.
- Related Reading Acts 2:22-47.
- Questions marked with an* are key questions on the passage.

A: Which part of the Chapter specially spoke to you?

B: Mary. 1*: Why is it important that Scripture is an eye witness account?

2: Which parts of the Bible could only Mary have known?

3: Have you ever received a promise from God which has taken many years to fulfil?   Luke 2:25-35.

C: The Church.   4*: Can a person be a Christian without being part of a local Church? What did Jesus say?   Mt 16:18, Heb 12:23.

5: Why did Jesus establish the church?

6*: What is the confession all Christians have in common?

7: Does the call of your family conflict with the call of God's family? Can you give any examples?

8: Why do some people feel faith is more important than church?

9: Do I enjoy or endure the fellowship of God's people?

D: The Holy Spirit.

10: Is the Church the place where I meet with the Holy Spirit?

11*: What would a Spirit filled service look like? Eph 5:18f 1Cor

A Prayer: - Father, we are beginning to see that Jesus did not only die to forgive our sins, but to make us a part of your family the church. Forgive us when we have criticised your people and despised the house of prayer. Help us to show the same devotion to your people as we have for you. You love your church; in Jesus name we ask that you would send us a spirit of renewal. Fill us with your Holy Spirit that we may be inspired with ideas and dreams that are part of your renewing fire. Grant us the vision to see what your church can be, and the faith to follow it through. Amen.

Memory verse week two: - *Matt 16:16+18.* *"Simon Peter answered; Thou art the Christ, the Son of the living God. -- Jesus answered -- Upon this rock I will build my church; and the gates of hell shall not prevail against it." KJV.*

Action Point: -

- Go home and seek God for a new filling of the Holy Spirit.
- Be committed in love to God's people, in your local church.
- "Let us not give up meeting together, as some are in the habit of doing, but let us encourage one another" Heb 10:25.

Activity for the whole Church: -

- Take a bowl a towel and a jug, if you wish you may wash the feet of a member of the congregation. Otherwise pour water into the bowl and place it at the foot of the cross.

- **Verses to read out.** *John 13:4-5 + 13-15, 'Jesus rose from supper, and laid aside his garments; He took a towel, and girded himself. After that he poured water into a basin, and began to wash the disciples' feet, and to wipe them with the towel. [Then He said] you call me Master and Lord: and so I am. If I then, your Lord and Master, have washed your feet; you also ought to wash one another's feet. KJV modernised.*

A New Hope.

Luke 23:43

"Jesus said unto him, Verily I say unto thee, today shalt thou be with me in paradise." KJV

A New Hope, for an old thief! (Luke 23:32-43.)

- It began with mockery. Matthew 27:44.

What changed his mind?

1. He saw Christ's innocence! Luke 23:41, John 18:38, 19:6.

2. He saw Christ as King. John 19:19, Lk23:42.

3. He knew Christ had the power to forgive. Luke 23:34, John 3:18-19, Mk 16:16.

The Unrepentant thief. Heb 4:7, John 6:44.

(His attitude to life sealed his death.)

The Repentant thief. A Genuine Repentance?

1. He knew death was not the end. V42.

2. He feared God. V40.

3. He confessed his sin. V41. (CF 1Jn 1:9-10.)

4. He confessed Jesus. V42.

5. He saw Christ's Power.

6. He asked for mercy and received a promise. V43.

3: A New Hope.

Luke 23:43

"Jesus said unto him, Verily I say unto thee, today shalt thou be with me in paradise." **KJV**

New Hope for an old thief!   (Luke 23:32-43.)

When Jesus offered paradise to the dying thief, he could not join the Church, yet the place in Heaven of the repentant thief is no less certain than Mary's. It seems only right that Jesus should reach out to Mary and bring her into the Church, but the account of the repentant thief shows us that even if we are far from God, we are not too far for him to reach us if we will change our hearts.

He was neither pure of heart nor religious; and we are told that he began the day insulting Christ through his bitterness and pain. *Matt 27:44 "In the same way the robbers who were crucified with him also heaped insults on him."* Yet as he witnesses Christ's death he moves from mockery to faith. Just before His death, Jesus promises him, ***"Tonight you will be with me in paradise" Luke 23:43.***

What changes his mind? Three things changed his mind. He saw **Jesus was innocent**, he saw **He was a King**, about to come into his kingdom, and he saw **He could offer him forgiveness.**

Somehow this man understands who Jesus really is. He may have heard Christ preach, he has certainly heard about him because he says *"this man has done nothing wrong"* Luke *23:41.* He recognises the character of Jesus, *"innocent"* of any crime. Pilate affirmed this when he twice said *"I find no basis for a charge against him" (John 18:38).* When the mob clamoured for blood, Pilate answered *"You take him and crucify him. As for me, I find no basis for a charge against him"* John *19:6.* Pilate knew that as a King, Christ was potential rival to Caesar. He also knew the Jewish leaders had rejected King Jesus. It was out of fear and jealousy that the Priests handed Jesus over to be crucified, not for any real crime. The thief, like Pilate, saw Christ's innocence.

He also saw the sign nailed above His head, *"JESUS OF NAZARETH KING OF THE JEWS,"* written in three languages, Hebrew the local language, Latin the legal language and Greek the universal language. It was as if Pilot did not want anyone to miss seeing who Christ was! It is there for the entire known world to read, for the thief to read, and for six hours on the cross the idea that Christ was King turned in his mind. At first he mocked with the other, *"Aren't you the Christ? Save yourself and us!"* Luke *23:39,* later he saw the door of the Kingdom, and said, "Jesus, remember me when you come into your kingdom" Luke 23:42.

He heard Jesus pray for his enemies, *"Father forgive them, they do not know what they are doing."* Somehow he became the only one at the cross to understand that Christ the King had the right to forgive sins. He wanted to be in Christ's Kingdom. In those few hours of crucifixion, he comes to a clear faith in Christ. He knows enough to call out to Christ, and he knows death will not be the end, for him or for Jesus. Suffocating and in agony he calls out, *"Lord, remember me when You come into Your kingdom" Luke 23:42 NKJV.*

The repentant thief should teach us clearly that salvation is by faith alone. The only thing he could contribute to his salvation was guilt. He is not a good or religious person, he cannot be baptised and admits he is guilty as charged. Yet the moment he puts his faith in Jesus he is fit for paradise. If we rely on our own goodness to take us into God's kingdom we will never get there, neither our sin nor our righteousness count before God, the only way to heaven is through faith in Christ. The Bible is clear on this, *John 3:18-19 Whoever believes in him is not condemned, but whoever does not believe stands condemned already because he has not believed in the name of God's one and only Son.* Jesus closing words in Matthews's gospel said, *"Whoever does not believe will be condemned" Mark 16:16.*

Faith in the crucified Christ is the one requirement necessary to be admitted to God's Kingdom.

The unrepentant thief: - Death bed repentance is possible; the first thief teaches us this, but it is very rare, we should never count upon being able to repent at the end of our lives. Anybody who decides to put off becoming a Christian till they are older will certainly never become a Christian. None can come to faith tomorrow, only today. We must respond when we are called, *Heb 4:7, "Today, if you hear his voice, do not harden your hearts".*

It is vitally important to realise that our attitude to our death is determined by our attitude to life. In the 1970s the island of Tenerife was a popular holiday destination, but it became the site of one of the world's worst air disasters. Planes had been diverted from Spain to the small Island airport, due to bad weather over Europe. As they lined up waiting their turn to depart, the weather worsened and more planes were redirected. Eventually one plane was taxiing for take off while another was trying to land. The planes struck each other with devastating violence and loss of life. Much of the disaster was caught on camera. One of the last men to escape from the taxiing aircraft became an international Christian speaker. He testified that as people tried to escape the flames, they did not call on God for help but in their panic swore and blasphemed against God. The manner in which they lived became the manner in which they died. If we live a life outside of faith in God, if cursing is common to us, then, we will die outside the faith of God with cursing, not prayer, on our lips. We die in the same manner in which we have lived. If we live a hurried life, always worrying about what we have to do next, we will die a troubled death worried about the things we have left undone. If we live with anger and bitterness we will die carrying that anger to the grave. If we don't care about life we will end up not caring about death. The famous last word's of John Wesley were "best of all God is with us" faith carried him through life and faith sustained him in death. The unrepentant thief lived and died in the bitterness of his sin; he died angry and cynical. Christ died trusting God the father when he said, "father, into your hands I commit my spirit." The repentant thief died trusting in Jesus. We will carry the attitudes we hold in life into our death. If we want to die the death of the righteous we must live the life of the righteous.

We need to put into our hearts and minds the principles and practices which will bring us in faith, to the door of God's kingdom. It is presumption to think we can put off having faith till a later date. If we do we may well find, that later we have hardened our hearts, and are no longer able to trust in God. Jesus said, *"No one can come to me unless the Father who sent me draws him," John 6:44.* If God draws us to follow him we need to respond positively, we do not know when He will draw us again. We should remember that there were two thieves upon the hill of Calvary, one died cursing and unrepentant, the other said *"We are punished justly, for we are getting what our deeds deserve. Lord, remember me when you come into your Kingdom."* Luke 23:42. Only one thief came to repentance, this should be a warning not to wait.

The Repentant thief, was it a genuine repentance? Many people are suspicious of 'death bed' repentance. At one time John Wesley doubted that a man could find peace on his death bed. He was only finally convinced when he ministered to a convict on death row in the prison at Oxford. They preached the message of faith and prayed with the man. Wesley writes, "He kneeled down in much heaviness and confusion, having no rest in his bones, by reason of his sins. After a space he rose up, and eagerly said, "I am now ready to die, I know Christ has taken away my sins; and there is no condemnation fore me." This was 27th April 1738; it proved to him that sudden conversion was possible and led him within a month to find Christ as his own saviour.

How do we know that the repentant thief was genuine? His words and actions prove his faith. Six things show us his faith, each of them is recorded Luke 23:39-43.

1, He knew that death was not the end of his existence; he

believed he had an eternal soul. Even after Jesus death he expects to be *remembered*. His faith said that this man can help me even from beyond the grave.

2, He *feared God*, which means he knew after he died he would face God's judgement. *"Don't you fear God," he said, "since you are under the same sentence? (v40)* He is acknowledging God's right as Judge.

3, He admitted his own sin. This is essential for every convert, we should be willing to admit our sin and see the perversion of sin in others, when it raises its head. He both confessed his sin and rebuked his companion. *"We are punished justly, for we are getting what our deeds deserve. But this man has done nothing wrong" (v41).* On the cross a change had come over him. Confession is always the road to cleansing. *1 John 1:9-10, "If we confess our sins, he is faithful and just and will forgive us our sins and purify us from all un-righteousness."*

4, He confessed Jesus, and placed his faith in him, saying *"he has done nothing wrong, and remember me."* This was his only hope, this innocent man dying beside him was about to enter his Kingdom.

5, He realised Jesus had the power to admit anyone he wished to His Kingdom, by implication he called Him King and openly proclaimed Jesus is *"Lord."*

6, He threw himself upon Christ's mercy, if Christ had forgiven His executioners surely He could forgive him.

He has no hope in himself, he knows his deeds are evil; he has no hope in this world' he is about to die; his only hope is that Christ will remember him. When Christ is our only hope we are in safe hands. He became the first person saved through faith in a crucified Lord. Though he had been genuinely wicked, he received the promise of salvation, confirmed by the word of God himself, *"today you will be with me in paradise."* The moment life left his body; he stood in God's paradise as one of the redeemed. If we follow the same steps that the dying thief took, we can be assured of the same welcome. We should realise that death is not the end and fear the God who has the right to judge us. We should confess our sin and place our faith in Jesus as Lord. We must realise he alone has the keys to the kingdom Heaven. Years later Jesus speaking to John on the Island of Patmos said *"I am the Living One; I was dead, and behold I am alive for ever and ever! And I hold the keys of death and Hades" Rev 1:18.* We should throw ourselves on his mercy, and do it today, knowing if we put it off we will never do it at all.

One thief perished, his sin dragging him to the grave. The other looked to Jesus and found paradise. When we come to faith, the door of heaven is open, but we still have a life of service to offer before we pass through that door. The Scripture promises us a life span of 70 to 80 years, *Ps 90:10 'The length of our days is seventy years-- or eighty, if we have the strength; yet their span is but trouble and sorrow, for they quickly pass, and we fly away.* We should plan on a life time to serve Christ, but be ready TO MEET HIM tomorrow. How many years do you have left IF God grants between 70 to 80 years? Christ's last words teach us forgiveness is through faith alone, but warn us not to squander that gift of life or faith. If we harden our hearts we too can miss the grace of God.

Week Three: Study Questions.

Suggested Hymns and songs are in the appendices p150.

- Group study reading: Luke 23:26-43.
- Related reading: Revelation 22:1-14.
- Questions marked with an* are key questions on the passage.

You do not have to cover all the questions.

A: Which part of the chapter specially spoke to you?

B: On Forgiveness.

1*: Why do we need to see that Christ was an innocent/sinless victim? (This links to the O.T. sacrifices to Christ Himself)

2: Do we sometimes think God cannot forgive us or others? Why?

3: If Christ is King, where is His Kingdom? John 18:37 + 19:19.

4: What one thing do we need in order to enter His Kingdom?

C: On Repentance.

5*: Do we agree that our attitudes in life will affect our attitude to death?

6: What practical steps can we take to change our attitudes?

7*: What are the different marks of genuine Christian conversion?

8: What message do the thieves bring to us?

9: How long do you still have to follow Christ? See Psalm 90:10. What steps should you take to grow as a disciple?

10: What are the signs of a hardened heart?

A Prayer.

Saviour, as we pray "remember me," may we also count our days correctly and give them back to you. While we wait for the final coming of your kingdom, may we serve you faithfully; keep us from falling. Forgive us that we so often think the things of this world are so important. We are beginning to understand that as we live, so shall we die, may we live under your guidance and grow in holiness so that when we do step through the door of your Kingdom we may not be ashamed. We ask this through the love and mercy of Jesus our Lord, Amen.

Memory verse week Three: - *Rom 10:9-10* **"That if you confess with your mouth, "Jesus is Lord," and believe in your heart that God raised him from the dead, you will be saved. For it is with your heart that you believe and are justified, and it is with your mouth that you confess and are saved.**

Action point: -

- What must I do to deepen my faith in Christ?
- Am I making excuses not to meet with God's people?
- Will I take my faith in hand and join in worship this week?

- Who can I invite to be part of God's family the Church?

Activity for the whole church: -

- First take a purple robe and drape it over the cross, then write up a label and nail it to the top of the cross. If you have more than one nationality in the church, it should be in English and the two other major languages. The label should read as follows: *"Jesus of Nazareth, the King of the Jews."*

- **Verse to read.** John 19:19-20 *'Pilate also wrote a title and put it on the cross; it read, "Jesus of Nazareth, the King of the Jews." Many of the Jews read this title, for the place where Jesus was crucified was near the city; and it was written in Hebrew, in Latin, and in Greek.'* *RSV*

The Great Cry of Dereliction.

"My God, my God, why have you forsaken me?" Mt 27:46.

The Curse of Darkness. (V 45) Is 63:3, Ex 10:21-23.

The Message in the darkness.

- To Israel. John 12:35-36.
- To establish the New Covenant. (Mt 27:45 Deut 21:22-23.)
- To prove Christ was cursed. (Joshua 7, 1Sam 15, Gal 3:13, 2Cor 5:19+21)
- The Scapegoat. Lev 16:7-10. Eph 4:9, 1Pet 3:19.

God's Judgment on Sin.

- (Rom 6:23, Ezek 18:20, Rom 3:23+26.)

God's Judgment on Christ.

- A Rend in the heart of God.
- Abandoned by the Father.

How did Christ Respond?

- Strength from the Psalms. Ps 22:1-2
- Calling on God. *"My God."* (CF Luke 22:42-43.)
- Seeing the resurrection? (A Psalm of Hope. Ps 22:14-20 + 24.)

How did the Crowd Respond? Mt 27:49.

- Ignorance & Fascination. (Malachi 4:5, Luke 1:17)

His Great Deliverance.

- A New Exodus. (Luke 9:30f, Eph 4:8f, 2Co 5:21.)

4: The Great Cry of Dereliction.

Matthew 27:45-54.

'And about the ninth hour Jesus cried with a loud voice, saying, Eli, Eli, lama sabachthani? that is to say, My God, my God, why hast thou forsaken me?'

Matt 27:46 KJV

As the hours pass and the Old Testament sacrifices are fulfilled and ended in Christ, the full weight of human sin, descends upon His shoulders, and Jesus is abandoned to the fate of the God forsaken. The darkness and brooding evil of sin, is mirrored in the darkness which covered the land. This is no eclipse; it is a tangible, spiritual, fearful darkness. Evil gathers over the head of Christ and God the father withdraws, leaving God the son to bear sin alone. Wesley views Jesus as the sin bearer, "See all your sins on Jesus laid: The Lamb of God was slain, His soul was once an offering made, for every soul of man." Isaiah said, *"He trod the wine press alone" Is 63:3.*

The message in the darkness: - A warning for those who reject Christ that judgement is following!

This is not the first time there was a curse of darkness. God sent darkness as a sign to Pharaoh in Egypt. *Ex 10:21-23 "Then the LORD said to Moses, "Stretch out your hand toward the sky so that darkness will spread over Egypt--darkness that can be felt." So Moses stretched out his hand toward the sky, and total darkness covered all Egypt for three days. No one could see anyone else or leave his place for three days. Yet all the Israelites had light in the places where they lived."* Egypt saw God's miracles and resisted His will, she endured darkness for three days; Israel say Christ's miracles resisted God's will & endured the Judgement of darkness for three hours while Christ died.

The Darkness was message to the nation of Israel. *Matt 27:45, "From the sixth hour until the ninth hour darkness came over <u>all the land</u>."* This was a symbol of God's displeasure upon a nation which had rejected the Christ. John tells us that, *"He came to His own, and His own did not receive Him" John 1:11-12 NKJV.* They rejected Christ and Judgement fell! The temple was destroyed and Israel was dispersed as a nation for 1900 years. The leaders of Jerusalem rejected Christ and the darkness symbolised this rejection. Jesus said to the Pharisees, *"If you were blind, you would not be guilty of sin; but now that you claim you can see, your guilt remains. John 9:41*

This unnatural sign proclaims, "If you reject the light of the world, you will walk in darkness" (John 12:35-36). Yet this truth does not only apply to Israel. Today we boast of computers in every home, yet we cannot even live in harmony with our neighbour, or even our family. We boast great advancements

57

and knowledge on one side, with nations in chaos and marriages in turmoil on the other. Many seem to have money without love, and knowledge, without faithfulness. If we reject the light of life in Jesus Christ, we will walk in darkness even though our knowledge increases. The darkness in today's western society is no better or worse than any other society throughout history, it is simply a symptom of the darkness in our own hearts; society reflects the dominant beliefs of the majority of its citizens. If our hearts are full of God we will act in honourable and loving ways, if they are full of selfishness and darkness we will not. The leaders of Jerusalem rejected Christ and the darkness that Israel experienced symbolised this rejection. If we too continue to reject Him we will also face judgement.

A Message to the world: - a message of hope, for those who accept Christ, God is establishing a New Covenant, a Covenant for all nations.   The "Old Covenant" under Moses was established with miracles and a mighty deliverance, so the "New Covenant" in Jesus is confirmed with miracles and a mighty deliverance. The supernatural darkness, the tearing of the curtain in the Temple, the earthquake that followed Christ's death (Mt 27:54) and the greatest deliverance of all, the resurrection from the dead, all proclaim that God is doing something new; He is establishing his "New Covenant." J C Ryle said, "Signs like these, on special occasions -- are a part of God's way in dealing with man. He knows the desperate stupidity and unbelief of human nature – (So through miracles) He compels men to open their eyes." The three hours of Darkness at midday should make us ask, what does this mean?

Problem for the Priests: - The Priests; they believed it was a sin to execute a man during the hours of darkness. The body had to be removed from the cross before the sun went down, their Law commanded it. *Deut 21:22-23 "If a man guilty of a capital offence is put to death and his body is hung on a tree, you must not leave his body on the tree overnight. Be sure to bury him that same day, because anyone who is hung on a tree is under God's curse. You must not desecrate the land the LORD your God is giving you as an inheritance?"* They believed that execution by public hanging was an open proclamation of God's curse upon the criminal, but that if he remained on the tree overnight the land would be desecrated by the act.

Carrying the Curse: - **This brings us to the third and deepest reason for the hours of darkness: By hanging Christ upon a tree, the leaders wanted to prove he was not the Messiah. It was not enough to have Jesus stoned to death like Stephen, or beheaded like James, if he was hung upon a tree, all the people would know that he was cursed by God; they believed He would be shown to be a false Messiah!**

Christians do not deny that Christ was cursed; Christ's cry of dereliction is the cry of the cursed. *"My God, my God, why have you forsaken me?"* To be cursed by God, means to be judged and condemned by Him as guilty and to suffer the punishment of that guilt. In the Old Testament Cursed things were designated "Korban" which means, to be handed over to God for total destruction. This curse was uttered against the village of Jericho; Achan disobeyed the curse of Korban and was destroyed along with his stolen goods (cf Joshua 7). Later in King Saul's day the curse was uttered against the Amalakites (1Samuel 15). To be cursed of God means to be God forsaken, and handed over to destruction, to be utterly hopeless!

To see Christ as cursed should raise questions for us. Doesn't God only punish the guilty? Was Christ punished for some failure? How could God punish His son? Did he not love Jesus? Why did he not save him? Was he really cursed of God? If we understand the Christ was truly cursed, we need to understand why! The answer is that Christ was suffering the curse of God, so that all who believe in Him would never have to face the curse of God. He has become our substitute, He is God forsaken so that we will never be forsaken by God. The idea that Christ should be God forsaken, and handed over to destruction has become for believers their means to eternal life. *Gal 3:13 "Christ redeemed us from the curse of the law by becoming a curse for us, for it is written: "Cursed is everyone who is hung on a tree."* This is the central teaching of the New Testament.

The fact that we have broken God's Law, expressed in the Ten Commandments, means that we stand guilty and under His curse. We are now at the heart of the mystery of the cross. There is a divine exchange being transacted here. Our sin is laid on Christ; our curse is born by him. The sinless one is counted guilty and we the guilty ones are set free. The Bible puts it this way, *"God was reconciling the world to himself in Christ, not counting men's sins against them. -- God made him who had no sin to be sin for us, so that in him we might become the righteousness of God" 2Cor 5:19+21.* The sin of all the ages is literally and spiritually placed on Christ. He becomes the Lamb of God, slain from the foundation of the world, the Scapegoat, the Divine sin bearer.

The Scapegoat. The Old Testament concept of "a Scapegoat" comes from Leviticus 16:7-10. Two goats were chosen, one was sacrificed as a sin offering, and the other was released into the wilderness. The Priest would place his hand upon the goats, and symbolically pass the sin of the people into the animals. Both animals would bear the sins of the people, one to death, becoming the blood sacrifice; the other would be released into the burning desert, forsaken by God; it symbolically carried the sins of the people into the fire of Hell.

1. Christ gave his life as the final sacrifice for sin.

2. He bore our sin on the cross becoming a blood sacrifice.

3. He bore our sin to the grave, becoming our representative in death.

4. Then He bore our sin beyond the grave, to the place of punishment itself. (Eph 4:9, 1Peter 3:19)

5. Finally he arose leaving sin in the grave an offering forgiveness to all who will come.

The only morally and spiritually pure man who ever lived, exchanged places with us, as the Scapegoat did with the people of Israel. In that moment God who hates sin turned from Christ, and He cried, *"My God, My God, why have you forsaken me?"* God's judgement for sin fell on him and by His stripes we are healed *1 Peter 2:24.* Christ literally became accursed for us.

God's Judgement on Sin: - We need to be as clear about this as we can.

1: - God must punish sin, He must punish it because He is absolutely holy, and He must punish it because sin is an offence against His Lordship in our lives. (All sin has at its heart self-centredness and a denial of God's right to rule our lives) If God leaves sin unpunished, He is neither just nor holy. His laws demand justice, His character guarantees justice. All sin must be punished whether thoughts, or words, or deeds.

2: - The animal sacrifices of the Old Testament teach us the serious consequences of sin. An innocent victim was sacrificed in place of the one who had sinned. The sacrificial lamb became a substitute for the penitent worshipper, and because it had died they would not die for their sin.

3: - The New Testament spells out that punishment which sin deserved, Rom *6:23 "the wages of sin is death."* In God's eyes sin deserves death, that death is both physical and spiritual. *Ezek 18:20, "The soul that sins, it shall die."* We are speaking here of eternal or soul death. God, who cannot lie, has promised that all who sin will die eternally. This leaves a dilemma, because all of us have sinned. *"All have sinned and fall short of the glory of God" Rom 3:23.* The only conclusion the Bible allows is that before God the whole world stands guilty of sin and under his sentence of death, physically and spiritually.

4: - God's laws demands our punishment, His justice guarantees our punishment but God's love demands mercy. God's solution is to supply a substitute, an innocent sacrifice, who will bear the punishment of our sin. Christ alone is that sacrifice, God who must punish sin places the punishment on him. God's holiness and justice are satisfied, sin has been punished and we may be forgiven. *Rom 3:26 "He did it to demonstrate his justice --- so as to be just and the one who justifies those who have faith in Jesus."* God has both punished sin and provided forgiveness.

The only thing we are called to do is to have faith in Christ, our saviour from sin. As the worshipper placed his hand on the scapegoat, we must reach out with faith and place it firmly in Christ. There are only two choices, we either pay for our own sin, which means eternal death, or find someone else who can pay the price. Only Christ can pay for sins! Only He was morally pure, a spotless sacrifice.

God's Judgement on Christ: - This means that Jesus separation from God was real, for the first time in eternity there was a rend in the heart of the Godhead. We cannot fully understand this; but when sin was placed upon the Son of God, he actually became that sin, and experienced abandonment by the Father. The Father forsook the Son and treated him as if he were the vilest of sinners. In the same way he will abandon all who refuse to repent and put their faith in Christ. Christ is God's remedy for sin, enabling God to judge sin and forgive the sinner. The tear in the Temple curtain was a symbol of the tear in fellowship at the heart of God, and a picture of the door to God which now stands open. As the Temple curtain was torn apart revealing the pathway into the Holy place, so the tear in the heart of God reveals the path we must tread. We enter God's presence through that torn curtain, through the broken body of Christ. *Heb 10:19-20 "Therefore, --- we have confidence to enter the Most Holy Place by the blood of Jesus, by a new and living way opened for us through the curtain,*

64

that is, his body." As the fellowship between Father and Son was broken, our fellowship with God was restored.

Christ endured the full punishment of Hell in the hours of darkness. *1 Peter 2:24 "He himself bore our sins in his body on the tree, so that we might die to sins and live for righteousness; by his wounds you have been healed."* Though Hell is depicted as a place of flame and torment, in reality it means being excluded from the presence of the love of God. Hell is living in the place where only God's justice is known. It is a place of utter loneliness, where we are forsaken by love. It is living with constant remorse, knowing that it was our own twisted heart that kept us from God's love. The cry of dereliction shows that Jesus was excluded from the presence of God, and endured the judgement of separation from God, which is Hell itself.

How did Jesus respond to this torment?

The physical torment was bad enough but the Spiritual torment was immeasurable. He responds by drawing strength from the words of Scripture. *Ps 22:1-2 "My God, my God, why have you forsaken me? Why are you so far from saving me, so far from the words of my groaning?"* Christ's cry is a direct quotation of Psalm twenty two. We need to notice that he is no longer calling God his Father, which was how he had always addressed him. That relationship has been set aside. As our representative He now calls out *"My God, my God."* This is the supreme act of faith, God has turned from the Son, but the Son has not turned from God. He may be abandoned and forsaken, but He still sees God's final purpose, to Jesus God is still *"MY God."* Even when He is forsaken he will not turn from God's purposes. Jesus does not simply say why? With his dying breath, He is saying, "I do not fully understand this suffering, but God is still My God and I will do his will."

This takes us back to Gethsemane, where Jesus said, *"Father, if you are willing, take this cup from me; yet not my will, but yours be done" Luke 22:42-43.* He is now living out the decision he made there.

Psalm 22 which Jesus is quoting accurately portrays the crucifixion: written 1000 years before the event, it tells of a man who is:

- *"poured out like water, and all his bones are out of joint:*
- *Whose heart is like wax; it is melted in the midst of his bowels.*
- *Whose tongue cleaves to His mouth.*
- *He is brought to the dust of death.*
- *Who is surrounded by wicked men.*
- *They pierced his hands and feet.*
- *And all his bones can be counted.*
- *They look and stare upon Him.*

- *They gamble for His clothes.* *Ps 22:14-20 (KJV)*

Yet it is still a Psalm of hope and faith, the Psalmist also proclaims.

- *You have answered Me. I will declare Your name to My brethren; In the midst of the assembly I will praise You. v 21f*
- *"He has not despised or disdained the suffering of the afflicted one; he has not hidden his face from him but has listened to his cry for help." Ps 22:24*
- *All the ends of the world shall remember and turn to the LORD, and all the families of the nations shall worship before You. NKJV*

Jesus clearly saw Himself fulfilling the prophecy of this Psalm, through the pain; Jesus saw the victory the Psalmist prophesied. He saw that the ends of the earth would come to God through the sacrifice He was making. Where do we look in our hour of need? We will never suffer as a sin bearer but can find strength in Scripture, what ever circumstance we find ourselves in.

How did the crowd respond?

With a mixture of ignorance and fascination! When Christ called God's name *"Eli"* they thought he was summoning Elijah. We know this because when he asks for a drink, the crowd say, *"Now let him alone, let us see if Elijah comes to save him"* Mt

27:49. Something grotesquely macabre is happening here. They knew the prophecy which said, that before the Messiah comes, Elijah must return. (Malachi 4:5) They reasoned if Elijah does come then Jesus must be the Messiah. One commentator feels the soldier gave him a drink just to keep him alive till Elijah came. Yet if Elijah had come, in a chariot of fire, what would they have done? They simply stood by, watching with a strange fascination. They didn't realise that the Spirit of Elijah had already come upon John the Baptist, (Luke 1:17) and that Elijah himself had appeared with Christ on the mount of transfiguration (Luke 9:30-31).

His Great Deliverance.

The conversation on the mountain had been about Christ's departure or "Exodus" which he was about to fulfil at Jerusalem. The Bible never depicts Christ's death as the end; it is an Exodus, a great deliverance. Just as the first Exodus brought God's people out of slavery in Egypt, into a promised land, so Christ's Exodus leads people out of slavery to sin, into the heavenly kingdom. This Exodus is accomplished by his death, resurrection and ascension. There is even a most unusual foretaste of this great deliverance from death given to us in Matthew's Gospel. *Matt 27:50-53 "When Jesus had cried out again in a loud voice, he gave up his spirit. At that moment the curtain of the temple was torn in two from top to bottom. The earth shook and the rocks split. The tombs broke open and the bodies of many holy people who had died were raised to life. They came out of the tombs, and after Jesus' resurrection they went into the holy city and appeared to many people."* What happened to these resurrected souls later we are not told, but it would seem probable that they accompanied Christ in the ascension as he returned to His Father in Heaven. Eph 4:8-10 tells us that, *"When He ascended on high, He led captivity captive, and gave gifts to men." (Now this, "He ascended"-- what does it mean but that He also first descended into the lower parts of the earth?) NKJV*

One Easter I showed the crucifixion scene from Jesus of Nazareth, to a group of 130 school children. The reactions were interesting. Some were visibly moved, others were fascinated by the spectacle. Some asked searching questions about what happened and how unfair it was. Others made jokes and asked why we celebrated by giving chocolate eggs. The same reactions which gathered round the cross that first Easter, still gather when the cross is experienced today. The film "The passion of The Christ" again provoked the same reactions as that first Good Friday: some derided, some scoffed, some wept, some worshipped and some did not understand. Our reaction to the cross is crucial, it defines our faith, and it is the pivotal moment in the life of Christ. He did not come simply to teach but to *"give his life as a ransom for many."* Mark 10:45.

At the cross we either mock or worship, the **cross should not appal us it should astound us,** the lengths to which God went to win back the world he loves. This was Jesus abandoned by God, rejected in death, so that we could be accepted. In those hours of darkness he bore our sin by becoming cursed, so that we could become righteous before God (2Cor 5:21). An Easter hymn puts it this way: "There was no other good enough, to pay the price of sin, He only could unlock the gate of heaven and let us in." Our reaction to the cross will determine our eternal destiny, either Christ bears the curse of the Law or we will bear it ourselves (Gal 3:13). Another Hymn: - I need no other sacrifice I need no other plea it was enough that Jesus died, and that He died for me." Is Christ your saviour? Trust him today!

The Spectacle.

What did you awake to see?
A crowd gathered for a tournament, a 'Grand National' event,
With gasps, and cries and gain and loss?

What did you rise up to see?
(One a penny, two a penny, hot cross buns)
Chocolate served in a foil shroud,
and the essence of life dripping away?

What did you go out to see?
A victim - a victory - a man? Yes and more than a Man!
God's humility, the eternal exchange,
Sin paid on the nail.

To what will you arise today?
Dark eyes forsaken on a crucifix, a putrid crime
or an invitation to paradise?

As fresh from the tomb Jesus speaks,
"I am the resurrection and the life. He who believes in me will
live, even though he dies; and whoever lives and believes in me
will never die." John 11:25-26

Week Four: Study Questions.

- Suggested songs may be found in the appendices p150.
- Group reading: Matthew 27:35-50.
- Related reading: Psalm 22. What references to the cross can you see in this Psalm?
- Questions marked with an* are key questions on the passage.

You do not have to cover all the questions.

Which part of the chapter specially spoke to you?

1: What lessons do you see in the hours of darkness?

2: What are the differences & similarities between the two Covenants?

3*: In what way was Christ cursed? Gal 3:13, Deut 21:22 - 23.

4: How does God judge sin? How does God forgive sin?

5*: What was the role of the scapegoat? Lev 17:7 – 10.

6: What punishment does God declare for sin? Rom 3:23 – 26.

7*: What dilemma did God seem to face before the cross?

8*: Why does Jesus not call God Father?

9: Where specifically was the curtain? Heb 10:19-20.

10*: What does the torn curtain symbolise?

11: Where did Jesus draw his strength from? Where do we turn in times of need?

12: What different attitudes have you observed to the cross?

13: What reaction do you have to the cross?

14: What do you make of the people resurrected from their graves? Matt 27:50 – 53, Eph 4:8.

15: Does the cross appal or astound you? Why?

A Prayer.

When darkness fills our hearts and clouds our vision, may we ever know that in Christ we are free from condemnation. We cannot fully understand it, but we believe that the judgement of God the Father fell on Jesus the Son. Because He faced the curse of God, we will be freed. Today we accept with humility and gratitude that it is by His stripes that we are healed. And we worship as we proclaim, "His blood can make the foulest clean, His blood availed for me." **Thanks** *be to God* **Amen.**

Memory verse week Four: - *Gal 3:13 "Christ hath redeemed us from the curse of the law, being made a curse for us: for it is written, Cursed is every one that hangs on a tree:" KJV*

Action point: -

- What can you do this week, to bring light into the darkness of someone who may feel abandoned?
- Thank God this week that you are loved and forgiven!
- Resolve in your heart and mind, to **never give up**, because you know that, with God, there is always a way through any problem.
- If you fall into sin humble yourself and return in repentance to Christ.

Activity for the whole church on Sunday: -

- Take a whip of cords and throw it at the base of the cross, take a crown of thorns and place it over the head of the cross.

- **Verse to read:** *Matt 27:45-46 'Now from the sixth hour there was darkness over all the land unto the ninth hour. And about the ninth hour Jesus cried with a loud voice, saying, Eli, Eli, lama sabachthani? That is, My God, my God, why hast thou forsaken me?' KJV*

The last Words from the cross.

"I am Thirsty." John 19:28.

The Physical Suffering of Christ.

All is accomplished. V28.

- To Atone = (To Cover, wipe away, ransom by substitute.)
- The man who was God.

No accidental death. V28. (Rom 5:5-7, Gal 4:4-5)

- Planned and Prophesied. (Ps 69:21, the wine vinegar.)

"It is finished." John 19:30

The Proclamation of Victory. (Tetalesti, Paid in full.)

- Our Debt for Sin. (Col 2:13-15, Deut 5:7-18.)

The consequences of forgiveness.

- The removal of guilt. (Satan's role as tempter, & Slanderer.)
- The removal of fear.
- We are forgiven, John 19:24. (Justification.)
- We are Cleansed, Eph 2:25-27. (Sanctification.)
- Death's sting has been drawn. 1Cor 15:54-57.

"Father into your hands I commit my spirit." Jn 19:30, Lk 23:46.

New strength from the Psalms. Ps 31:5.

- A Restored Relationship (Father!) (CF Jn13:3)

The Cross did not kill Jesus. Mt 27:50

A Confidence in His Death. *"Surely this man was the Son of God." Mk 15:39, John 19:35.*

5: The Last Words from the cross.

(John 19:28-37)

Jesus has been on the cross for six hours. From noon to three o'clock he endured the terrible hours of darkness, as he bore the curse of the law and carried our sins. Now he calls out *"I am thirsty."* Is there significance in these simple words of suffering?

The Physical suffering of Christ. v28.

We should not ignore the physical suffering Jesus endured. Crucifixion was designed to keep the victim alive as long as possible, whilst producing the maximum amount of pain. The nerves, torn by the nails would pulsate with a terrible agony. The temperature of the victim's body would rise till dizziness and nausea took over. Every movement of the body would incite intense physical torture, tearing at the open wounds and cramping the muscles. As long as the victim could push upon the nails he could breathe, this is why the soldiers often broke the legs of the victim. Once he was unable to stand the pain of the nails, he would die of suffocation. A more drawn out and painful death is hard to imagine. Every breath was won in searing pain, and each word spoken would be in extreme effort. Yet even in his death, there was no self pity or bitterness in Jesus. The fact that he only spoke once about his own pain is quite incredible. With Jesus, there was no hint of self-centredness, not even in his death.

What is more, he did not display his own need until he knew *"that all was now accomplished."* What had been accomplished in these six hours? The answer is the salvation of all who would believe in him. Forgiveness had been bought and atonement had been made.

The idea of Atonement has three possible applications: 1, to cover over sin 2, to wipe away sin 3, to ransom by offering a substitute. In atoning for our sin Christ has not simply covered over our sins, or wiped them away, He has become our substitute and paid our debt.

Christ himself becomes the bridge between God and man. He dies as a man alone, under the curse of God. Jesus the man bears our sin. But as a man his sacrifice would not be enough. If Christ were simply man he would be tainted by sin, just like the rest of humanity. Yet he is not simply a man, he is the man who was God. As God he bears our sin into himself, and suffers the judgement that should have fallen on his lost creation. God the creator becomes part of Creation in order to bear our sin. Because Jesus the man has born my sin, he can represent me before God. Because Jesus as God has born my sin, he can offer forgiveness. Only a spotless sacrifice could be acceptable, and only God himself could supply that sacrifice in Christ; because only Christ was sinless. In Christ man and God are brought together, God himself bears our sin, and we may enter His holy presence without fear. Wesley wrote "His blood atones for all our race and sprinkles now the throne of grace." Nothing can be added to this salvation, He alone accomplished it, and all we can do is accept His atoning sacrifice.

We should also understand that ***Jesus spoke not because of His own pain but "so that scripture would be fulfilled."*** It was planned to the last detail, and prophesied in the Old Testament, even down to His calling for a drink. **This cry of thirst was part of the proof that Christ was the Messiah.** *Ps 69:21 "They put gall in my food and gave me vinegar for my thirst."* The wine mixed with gall, a drugged wine was refused, but he did accept the wine vinegar, which would have been part of the rations of the soldiers who stood guard at the cross. He took the wine vinegar, to quench his thirst so that he could speak one last time. His next cry was a proclamation. The wine was offered upon a sponge and *John 19:30* says, ***"When he had received the drink, Jesus said, "It is finished." With that, he bowed his head and gave up his spirit."***

It is finished. v30 The question is: "what is finished?" Was it the ordeal of the Cross? No! Christ is not saying it is all over,

I am about to die. This is a proclamation of victory. He knew his sacrifice had paid the full price of sin, but we did not. Usually a dying man has a very quiet voice but Jesus strengthened by the wine, proclaims to the entire world, that he has won!

John 19 v28 used this same word, **(tetalesti)** *"all was accomplished"* (NIV = completed) here in **Vs 30 the translation is** *"it is finished"*. This word comes from the world of commerce. When someone paid their debt "Tetalesti" would be written over the bill: "PAID IN FULL". Jesus understood that his death had paid a debt. It was not a debt He owed. It was the debt that we owed to the broken laws of God.

The Scripture is clear, each transgression standing against us, as if it were a written indictment. You have probably heard of the Lamb's Book of Life; you may not have heard of the book of our lives. *Rev 20:11-15 "I saw a great white throne and Him who sat on it, from whose face the earth and the heaven fled away. And there was found no place for them. And I saw the dead, small and great, standing before God, and books were opened. And another book was opened, which is the Book of Life. And the dead were judged according to their works, by the things which were written in the books. The sea gave up the dead who were in it, and Death and Hades delivered up the dead who were in them. And they were judged, each one according* to his works. *Then Death and Hades were cast into the lake of fire. This is the second death. 15 And anyone not found written in the Book of Life was cast into the lake of fire"* NKJV.

Paul tells us, *"He forgave us all our sins, having cancelled the written code, with its regulations, that was against us and that stood opposed to us; he took it away, nailing it to the cross."* *Col 2:13-15.* Our **debt was paid at the cross.** Each broken command stands against our account and the only payment acceptable is the sacrificial death of Christ, our saviour, and substitute. The commandments of the Old Testament were never a means of obtaining God's favour; if we break but one we are still classed as a law breaker. The truth is that the commandments measure our guilt; they do not proclaim our innocence. No living man, before Jesus, ever kept the commandments. All stood guilty of breaking God's laws. On the cross God not only saw his Son nailed there, He saw our sins nailed there with Him. The written code standing against us was nailed to the cross and we were set free. "Paid in full," said Jesus!

The Consequences of forgiveness: Now if Christ has taken the legal punishment for sin, then two things are true **1:** We do not need to be dominated by guilt. **2:** We need not fear death.

1, Satan's authority over us comes through guilt. His strategy is relentless. Satan wants to convince us that sin is

80

habitual and unavoidable. He will tempt us until we fall and then tell us we could not help it. Each moral failure becomes easier till sin becomes a habit. We become trained and ingrained in the habit of sinning; what we thought was enticing becomes enslaving.

If we do manage to resist temptation, his second ploy is guilt; to **accuse us of some past sin**, to keep us feeling useless and defeated. This way we will never feel we are able or worthy of serving Christ. If he cannot stop us believing in Christ he will seek to stop us serving Christ.

Guilt is his chief weapon. Once we are filled with guilt over our past we are depressed and ineffective. Our self confidence is rock bottom, and we feel worthless. His accusations ring true in our hearts and we even begin to believe we are a hopeless case. He slanders our name and our character, and then proves our weakness by offering further temptations. By now we are so discourage we reason that "If am that bad already, it doesn't matter if I sin." We have believed a lie, and argued ourselves into defeat; we fall to his temptation and become polluted by sin.

Now he really has us, we feel a deeper sense of guilt, and wonder why Christ ever loved us. We may even give up on our faith altogether, or else settle for a mediocre mundane Christian existence, which never satisfies us. We believe this is all we can expect, because we are so bad at being a Christian. Satan's power consists in temptation, accusation, guilt and slander. If we listen to his lies we will never progress with God. Guilt is crippling to spiritual growth, and it is deceptive because it focuses on our feelings and not on the fact of Christ's forgiveness.

Jesus has taken all of our sin, all the accusations against us are nailed to the cross (Col 2:14). This is justification. Our guilt is covered, and we do not need to wallow in it any more. God loves us, Christ has died for us; guilt has been removed and we have been pardoned. Taking away the accusations against us leaves the devil powerless. We may actually speak to the devil; his accusations are true, we agree, we have sinned, we are weak, but our guilt is atoned for, Christ has suffered in our place. We are free and guilt will not rule our hearts.

Where sin is no longer counted; the devil has no power to accuse us. We must learn to take our guilt to Christ and nail it to the cross. God does not want to show himself as our Judge, but as our loving heavenly father. Our sins are forgiven for Christ's sake, thanks be to God. *John 8:3, "If the Son therefore shall make you free, ye shall be free indeed" KJV.* As believers we are free to love God, we are free to be loved by God, we are free to serve God and if we do fall into sin we are free to repent and break free of sin's addictive habit.

But there is a second step; forgiveness is not the same as cleansing. Next God seeks to cleanse our hearts, to form within our being a lifestyle of holiness. This is sanctification the blood bought our forgiveness, but now that we are forgiven, we must walk according to His Word, in a new and clean life style.

The flow of blood and water from Christ's side speaks of forgiveness and cleansing. The Bible tells us that, *"Christ loved the church and gave himself up for her **to make her holy**, cleansing her by the washing with water **through the word**."* *Eph 5:25-27* Christ has not simply forgiven, he has cleansed us.

To help us stay clean we are given two powerful allies, 1: The word of God to feed us and, 2: the Sprit of God to empower us. Our calling is learn of His word, be led by His Spirit and stay near to the cross, so that if we do fall we quickly confess our sin. If we are to combat temptation, we need to be quick to confess, even our temptations, and eager to be filled with the Holy Spirit and resist the devil's suggestions. *James 4:7 "Submit yourselves therefore to God. Resist the devil, and he will flee from you* KJV. This is what is known as sanctification, growing in holiness through the combined ministry of the Word and the Spirit. Then when we are tempted, confessing the temptation before we fall.

2: The fear of death has been removed, because its sting has been drawn. Death is still an enemy, but not one which will not destroy us. Paul understood this, he wrote, *"then the saying that is written will come true: "Death has been swallowed up in victory." "Where, O death is your victory? Where, O death is your sting?" The sting of death is sin, and the power of sin is the law. But thanks be to God! He gives us the victory through our Lord Jesus Christ." 1Cor 15:54-57*

The problem is if we enter death bearing our own sin, then death has a sting in the tail. The laws we have broken are paraded before the face of a Holy God. Satan "the accuser," demands that the penalty of the law be exacted, and that penalty is eternal death. The moment we die, we will know exactly what we were really like. For Believer and non-believer, there will be no excuses, only a list of offences against the majesty of God. *2 Cor 5:10 "We must all appear before the judgment seat of Christ; that every one may receive --- , according to that he hath done, whether it be good or bad." KJV*

Now if someone took away that list, death would be toothless, its sting would have been drawn. This is what Jesus did, he took the list nailed it to the cross, and destroyed the power death has over us. For the Christian death can even be welcome, Paul came to this place when he said, *"I --- desire to depart, and to be with Christ; which is far better:" Phil 1:23 KJV*

Jesus has lifted the curtain on death showing us that it is not a place of darkness, but a place of welcome. For the forgiven will walk through death to eternal life. Which brings us to Jesus last cry, as He walks through the door of death; He utters a cry of Faith.

The Seventh Cry: Luke alone records the final prayer, as he bowed his head, "Jesus called out with a loud voice, "Father, into your hands I commit my spirit. "When he had said this, he breathed his last." Luke 23:4.

Jesus dies in complete trust. He no longer speaks of God as distant, once again the Father / Son relationship is restored. The great cry of dereliction was a quote from the psalms. Now again, as he breathes out his spirit, Jesus finds strength in the Psalms. He quotes *Ps 31:5, "Into your hands I commit my spirit"* He simply adds the word father. Sin has been born, forgiveness has been bought, and the relationship with the father has been restored. Earlier, as he carried our sin He was God forsaken. The essential unity between the Father and the Son had somehow been disrupted by sin; but now, in assurance of faith, He commits his spirit to his Father.

There is a certainty in these last words, John tells us, *"Jesus knew that the Father had put all things under his power, and*

that he had come from God and was returning to God;" John
13:3 He knew that death was not the end, and now in simple
surrender of faith places his Spirit in the hands of God. Where
Luke tells us Jesus breathed his last, **Matthew is clearer**, *"He*
yielded up his Spirit." Mt 27:50. **It was not the cross that**
killed our Saviour, He did not die from the wounds of the
executioner. *John 10:18 "No man takes (My life) from me, but*
I lay it down of myself. I have power to lay it down, and I
have power to take it again." KJV. Once his task was fulfilled,
He handed back His eternal Spirit to the Father and his body
breathed no more.

"Was it the nails, Oh Saviour? That bound Thee to the tree?
Nay, `twas Thine everlasting love, Thy love for me, for me.
Oh, make me understand it, Help me to take it in;
What it meant for thee the Holy One, to bear away my sin."
(Katherine AM Kelly)

Confidence in death.

There is a confidence in these last words of Jesus, which we
usually do not find in the face of death. The last words of a man
often reveal what kind of a person he was. When Cardinal
Mazarin (1602-1661) chief minister of France, was told he had
but two months to live, he was found wandering the corridors of
his palace mourning the loss of his beloved paintings. "Must I
quit all these" he said "farewell, my dear pictures that I love so

well and have cost me so much!" He was consumed with the love of art, but not the love of God. J P Morgan a financier, and one of the wealthiest men of his day was known to be a rough and impatient individual, his last words were "don't baby me so." A well known German composer died speaking the name Mozart. A restaurant owner died saying "Always slice the ham thin." These people warn us that what is important in our life will cling to us in our death. A Christian woman in her nineties, who had followed Christ for half a century, in her last sickness said, "tell the children that an old woman who is just on the borders of eternity, is very much grieved that she did not begin to love the saviour when a child. Tell them youth is the time to serve the lord." John Wesley's dying words were "best of all God is with us!" How we live will profoundly affect how we die.

Christ could trust his father on the cross because he had trusted him all his life. No man lived like Jesus, and no man died like Jesus, bearing the sins of the world. When the Centurion who oversaw the execution witnessed all that happened, and how Christ died, he was convinced and said, *"Surely this man was the Son of God" Mark 15:39*. What happened to Jesus is not simply a historic fact, it still affects us today.

We still sin, and we still die. Considering the cross should bring us to repentance and faith. These things were written down by the witnesses so that we may believe. John gives us the centurions testimony, *"He who has seen has testified, and his testimony is true; and he knows that he is telling the truth, so that you may believe." John 19:34-36 NKJV.* He also says, *"Truly Jesus did many other signs in the presence of His disciples, which are not written in this book; but these are written that you may believe that Jesus is the Christ, the Son of God, and that believing you may have life in His name." John 20:30-31 NKJV.* Our response to Christ's cries should be one of worship, *"truly, He was the Son of God."*

Having looked at the cross it is important that we too respond. Here is a prayer for anyone seeking to place their faith in Jesus.

Lord Jesus *I see now that you died for my sin. There was no sin in you, yet you offered yourself up an innocent sacrifice. I have lived as though your death meant nothing. Today I reach out my hand, as the priest did to the sacrificial animal, and place my sins on your head! I accept that my punishment fell on you. Thank you Lord that you died for me, I offer you my life today and pray that you will forgive my sin, cleanse my heart and mind, and make me a true disciple. You have said that you will never turn away anyone who comes to you, so today I come. Lord accept my life as I offer it to you, may I live now, no longer for myself but for your glory. Amen.*

Week Five: Questions for further study.

- Suggested songs and Hymns are in the Appendices p150.
- Group reading: Mark 15:33-47.
- See also the Centurion's story, Appendix 1.
- Related reading: Psalm 31: 1-18 or 24.
- Questions marked with an* are key questions on the passage.

Reflect on the Centurion's story.
You do not have to cover all the questions.

1: How do you react to Christ's physical and His spiritual sufferings?

2: What does the idea of atonement include?

3: Can we keep the 10 commandments? If not, then what is their purpose?

4*: Was the death of Christ inevitable?

5: What did the Cross accomplish?

6*: What are Satan's favourite schemes against believers? Which do you fall for?

7: What power does death still hold over people? 1Cor 15:53-57. Do we still fear death?

8: Have you met people who have died with great peace and grace?

9: What do the terms "justification" and "sanctification" mean?

10: Why did Jesus call God Father as He died?

11: What brought the centurion to faith? What does today?

12: What is our response to the cross of Christ?

A Prayer.

We have no idea what tomorrow will bring, nor when you will call us home. May we live as those who believe in the death and resurrection of our Lord Jesus Christ, may we die as those who are looking for a better Kingdom. Grant us grace that we may live this life by the eternal truths of your word and leave this life with the confession of faith on our lips, proclaiming "truly Jesus is the son of God". Amen.

Memory verse week Five: - *Col 2:13-14* **"God made you alive with Christ. He forgave us all our sins, having cancelled the written code, with its regulations, that was against us and that stood opposed to us; he took it away, nailing it to the cross."**

Action Point: -

- Be an encourager! What words of encouragement do you want to give to your family, or friends? Speak while you can!
- Is there any item I am attracted to more than Christ? Downsize, give it away or sell it and give the money away!
- Ask God who to share the message of the cross with?
- Have you made your will yet? Sort it out and don't let your family down!

Activity for the whole church: -

- Take three 6 inch nails and hammer them into the cross, one in the upright and two in the cross bar.

- **Verse to read**: *Gal 3:13 'Christ has redeemed us from the curse of the law, having become a curse for us (for it is written, "Cursed is everyone who hangs on a tree"). NKJV*

The Resurrection Fact or Fantasy?

(1Cor 15v3-8 + 12-20)

An age of cynicism.

The importance of the resurrection.

If it is not true!

- The Apostles are liars. V5 + 7
- The Bible can not be trusted.
- Our faith useless? V17
- Death is the end. V18
- Christians should be pitied. V19

The evidence for the resurrection.

What really happened? The Evidence!

Was Jesus really dead?   (Mk 15:37 + 23-24, Jn 19:32-33)

- Was the tomb empty? (Lk 23:55-56)
- The guards on watch. (Mt 27:62-66 + 28:11-15)
- The rumours of a body snatching. (Mt 28:11-15).
- Could the disciples really have stolen the body? (1 Sam 31:11-13, Mt 26:56, John 20:19)
- The change in the disciples. 1 Cot 15:5-7.

The significance of the resurrection.

- A people of faith. Heb 7:16.
- Death is not the end. (1Cor 15:20, Lk23:43, Ecc 12:7.)
- Our Sins are forgiven. (1Cor 15:17)
- The Bible can be trusted. (Lk 24:46-47, Acts 2:24 + 25:18-19, Rev 1:18)

6: The Resurrection Fact or Fantasy?

"I delivered unto you first of all that which I also received, - that Christ died for our sins according to the scriptures; And that he was buried, and that he rose again the third day according to the scriptures:"
1Corinthians 15:3-4 *KJV*

If we remain with the cross but disregard the resurrection, then we are only telling half the Easter story. On the cross our forgiveness was purchased, in the resurrection our freedom was proclaimed. So today, we move to the climax of the Easter story, the resurrection.

An age of Cynicism.

We live in days where miracles and supernatural events are viewed with scepticism. Even the resurrection, the greatest miracle of all has been under attack in recent years. David Jenkins the former Bishop of Durham felt that it was unimportant to believe in the physical bodily resurrection of Jesus. The Jehovah's witnesses teach that Christ did not physically rise, but his Ghost or spirit appeared to the disciples. The Moslem faith does not even believe Christ died, it teaches that he was caught away from the cross and someone else died in his place. It is no longer enough to simply proclaim the resurrection; when it comes to the miraculous, people demand proof. The question is have we any proof that a man called Jesus, 2000 years ago defeated death and returned from the grave?

The Apocryphal book of Ecclesiasticus says, *"Do not find fault before examining the evidence; think first, & criticise afterwards,"* this is wise advice. Christians are often accused of "blind faith", uncritically accepting something without examining it to see if it is true. This mindless belief is never encouraged in the Bible, it says, *"study to show yourselves approved to God". 2 Tim 2:15.* If we are not willing to look at the facts then we can be accused of being ostriches with our heads in the sand. If we examine the facts and they hold good, then it is not the Christians who are blind, but those who are unwilling to examine and believe the evidence.

The importance of the resurrection.

The Apostle Paul tells us of the importance of the resurrection. (1Cor 15:3-8 + 12-19) He clearly sees the resurrection as the foremost among Christian teachings. ***"What I received I passed on to you as of first importance: that Christ died for our sins according to the Scriptures, that he was buried, that he was raised on the third day according to the Scriptures." (v3)***

If the resurrection is not true, then there are very serious consequences for the Christian faith. Paul gives us five reasons showing us the importance of the resurrection.

1, If Christ is not raised then the Apostles are liars. This means we cannot trust anything else they say, because they all claim to have seen Jesus alive after the Crucifixion. *"He appeared to Peter, and then to the Twelve. --- Then he appeared to James, then to all the apostles, and last of all he appeared to me also, as to one abnormally born"* says the Apostle Paul. (V5 + 7) His conclusion is, if Christ has not been raised, *"we are then found to be false witnesses about God, for we have testified about God that he raised Christ from the dead".* (1Cor 15:15.) In fact Paul claims that seeing Christ alive after his death is one of the signs of a genuine Apostle. *1Cor 9:1, "Am I not an apostle? Have I not seen Jesus our Lord? Are you not the result of my work in the Lord?"*

2, If there is no resurrection then the Scriptures cannot be trusted. The death and resurrection of the Messiah was widely predicted in the Old Testament. When Peter speaks of the resurrection on the day of Pentecost, he quotes the Psalms. ***"Because you will not abandon me to the grave, nor will you let your Holy One see decay.*** *You have made known to me the path of life; you will fill me with joy in your presence, with eternal pleasures at your right hand."* **Ps 16:10-11.** The Prophet Isaiah also predicts the resurrection.

"See, my servant will act wisely; he will be raised and lifted up and highly exalted. Just as there were many who were appalled at him-- his appearance was so disfigured beyond that of any man and his form marred beyond human likeness-- so will he sprinkle many nations, and kings will shut their mouths because of him." **"After the suffering of his soul, he will see the light of life** *and be satisfied; by his knowledge my righteous servant will justify many, and he will bear their iniquities."* (Isaiah 52:13-15 & 53:11) What happened to Jesus was *"according to the Scriptures." (v3)* If we cannot trust them on the resurrection, then they are not to be trusted at all. The resurrection is the central fact of the New Testament; it is not presented as a belief or a feeling but as a historic fact.

3, Our faith is useless. Why? Because the Christian faith is basically very simple, it has one core premise, that I am a sinner and Christ has died for my sins. The resurrection is the proof that God accepted His sacrifice. So if Jesus did not rise, we cannot be sure of our forgiveness. *"If Christ has not been raised, your faith is futile; you are still in your sins."* (v17) In fact it is worse than this!

4, If Jesus did not rise then death is the end, nobody will rise, there is only oblivion / annihilation. *"If Christ has not been raised, --- Then those also who have fallen asleep in Christ are lost."* (v17-18) Jesus is declared to be the first one to defeat

96

death. The promise is that all who follow him will defeat death too. He is the first fruits of a glorious harvest. Here in Jersey as I write, the farmers are lifting the first Jersey Royal potatoes. These are the most valued and sought after of the crop, and the condition of the first of the crop is a pointer to what is to follow. 1Cor 15:20-22, *"But Christ has indeed been raised from the dead, the first fruits of those who have fallen asleep. For since death came through a man, the resurrection of the dead comes also through a man. For as in Adam all die, so in Christ all will be made alive."* The Bible is clear: because Christ is risen, we too will rise.

5, If there is no resurrection Christians should be pitied. They believe in a lie and hope for life after death when there is none. *"If only for this life we have hope in Christ, we are to be pitied more than all men."* (1Cor 15:19) Without the resurrection of Christ, the hope of heaven is just a fanciful illusion.

This is how important the Bible says the resurrection is. It is the validating fact of the Christian faith. *"Christianity stands or falls with the resurrection"* Adolph Harnack. If we do not believe that Christ rose then we have no basis for the Christian faith at all.

What is the evidence for the resurrection? Is it reliable?

What really happened? The first obvious question to ask is, was Jesus really dead? Many have felt that when Jesus was taken from the cross, he was not really dead. He had fainted through the extreme torture of the cross, but revived in the cool of the tomb. This has been described as the swoon theory. It has even been suggested that the spices used to embalm the body were actually there to restore him to health. The disciples nursed back to life the wounded Jesus, the rest is legend. Many have followed this theory including the poet D H Lawrence.

Was Jesus really dead? To answer this question we need to understand what happened on the cross. This was a common enough death and very effective. First the victim was whipped or scourged. He would be stripped and tied over the whipping post, and then the lectors would administer the scourging. The whip was made of leather thongs with bone, glass or lead fastened to its tips. The Jews limited their beatings with rods to 39 strokes; the Romans had no such qualms. Bishop Eusebius of Caesarea witnessed the process of whipping and describes it in his writings. The "veins were laid bare, and that the very muscles, sinews, and bowels of the victim were open to exposure." The man would be half dead before he ever approached the cross. From the record of the gospels we see that Jesus was so weakened by his flogging that he could not carry the cross himself, they had to conscript Simon from Cyrene to carry the cross.

In Mark 15:21-22, we are told they *"brought"* Jesus to the

place called Golgotha. It seems to indicate that at that point he was dragged or carried, not simply taken there. Following the flogging his strength could barley carry his own weight.

The cross was such a hideous death that no Roman citizen was ever crucified; only criminals from conquered nations were put to death on a cross. Cicero the Roman orator spoke of its utter horror. *"Even the word, cross, must remain far not only from the lips of the citizens of Rome, but their thoughts, their eyes, their ears"*. The cross itself was a method of torture, as much as death. The victim was publicly stripped and humiliated. To breathe he would have to pull upon the nails hammered through the wrists and push upon the nails fastening the feet. Each breath would be won at extreme pain. Often people suffered for days. This drawn out death was not planned for Jesus. John tells us, *"It was the day of Preparation, and the next day was to be a special Sabbath. Because the Jews did not want the bodies left on the crosses during the Sabbath, they asked Pilate to have the legs broken and the bodies taken down." John 19:31* The guards came to break the legs of the victims: this stopped them breathing and so finish the crucifixion. At the end of six hours of torment, Mark tells us *"with a loud cry he breathed his last"*. Jesus legs were never broken because the guards saw that he was already dead. After all this was Jesus alive?

The witnesses to the death of Jesus: Joseph of Arimathea, Pilate the Governor and the soldier on duty, all confirmed the death of Christ. Joseph, a member of the Jewish ruling council asked for the body of Jesus. He had been a secret disciple but now as Christ dies he comes openly for the body. Pilate checked that Jesus was dead before he released the body for burial. Mark 15:43-46 *"Joseph of Arimathea, a prominent member of the Council, who was himself waiting for the kingdom of God, went boldly to Pilate and asked for Jesus' body. Pilate was surprised to hear that he was already dead. Summoning the centurion, he asked him if Jesus had already died. When he learned from the centurion that it was so, he gave the body to Joseph."* (John 19:31-34)

The soldiers' testimony is irrefutable. *"The soldiers therefore came and broke the legs of the first man who had been crucified with Jesus, and then those of the other. But when they came to Jesus and found that he was already dead, they did not break his legs. Instead, one of the soldiers pierced Jesus' side with a spear, bringing a sudden flow of blood and water.* John was there as an eye witness, he saw the spear and the sudden flow of blood and water. Michael Green says, "This is evidence of massive clotting of the blood in the main arteries and especially strong medical proof of death. The blood and water from the spear thrust is proof positive that Jesus was already dead". Joseph was in no doubt; he embalmed the body with 75 lbs of spices and laid it in his own tomb. (John 20:39-

40) This was a lavish extravagance but it was not unusual. Myrrh was the common embalming substance and reminds us of the gifts given at Jesus birth. Aloes were used as a preservative and cleanser, a sweet smelling savour to act against the pungency of the Myrrh. Jesus was really dead. Pilate was surprised by it, the Roman soldier investigated it, and Joseph confirmed it. We need have no doubt about his death the Romans were expert at executions. Which brings us to the resurrection; **was the tomb really empty?**

1, The first evidence for the resurrection is **the empty tomb**; no one could find the body of Jesus. Some have argued that in their grief, the women went to the wrong tomb, and finding it empty assumed he had risen to life. Seeing someone, perhaps the gardener confirmed their suspicions, and in their excitement they thought Christ was alive. This suggestion is as ludicrous as it is insulting. The Gospels all agree. Luke 23:55-56 *"The women who had come with Jesus from Galilee followed Joseph and saw the tomb and how his body was laid in it. Then they went home and prepared spices and perfumes. But they rested on the Sabbath in obedience to the commandment."* It is very insulting to these devout women, to say they could not remember the burial place of the man they had followed as their Lord for three years. Their devotion is beyond doubt; they were coming to anoint his body. If they went to the wrong tomb, the authorities, Jewish or Roman, could simply point to the right tomb, show them the body and the rumour would be over.

2, **The guards** posted to the tomb give us further evidence. The very thought of a resurrection was **a problem for the rulers of the Jews.** They tried to make sure there could be no thought of a resurrection. Mt 27:62-66 *"the chief priests and the Pharisees went to Pilot. "Sir," they said, "we remember that while he was still alive that deceiver said, 'After three days I will rise again.' So give the order for the tomb to be made secure until the third day. Otherwise, his disciples may come and steal the body and tell the people that he has been raised from the dead. This last deception will be worse than the first." "Take a guard," Pilot answered. "Go; make the tomb as secure as you know how." So they went and made the tomb secure by putting a seal on the stone and posting the guard.* The Authorities took every precaution to stop the resurrection. "Vein the stone, the watch, the seal; Jesus burst the gates of hell".

When the Angel rolled the stone away, the guards were no use at all. The stone was not removed to let Jesus out, but to let the women in, so that they could witness the resurrection. *Matt 28:6 "He is not here; he has risen, just as he said. Come and see the place where he lay."*

3, **The rumour of body snatching** invented by the Jewish leaders to explain why the tomb was empty, also proves the resurrection. Matt 28:11-15 *"While the women were on their way, some of the guards went into the city and reported to the chief priests everything that had happened. When the chief priests had met with the elders and devised a plan, they gave the soldiers a large sum of money, telling them, "You are to say, 'His disciples came during the night and stole him away while we were asleep.' If this report gets to the governor, we will satisfy him and keep you out of trouble." --- And this story has been widely circulated among the Jews to this very day."* This story lasted a long time. Tertullian who was born AD 200 quotes it in his "Apology". "The grave was found empty of all but clothes, -- nevertheless, the leaders of the Jews, spread abroad a lie, -- that the body of Jesus had been stolen by his followers". John Chrisostom, AD 347-407 shows us that this lie really helps the Christian cause. "Indeed this establishes the resurrection; the fact of their saying the disciples stole him. For this is the language of men confessing, that the body was not there. When therefore they confess the body was not there, but the stealing of it is shown to be false and incredible, by the guard, by the seal, and by the timidity of the disciples, the proof of the resurrection --appears incontrovertible".

4, Could the disciples really have stolen the body?
There is an Old Testament precedent. 1 Sam 31:11-13 *"When the people of Jabot Gilead heard of what the Philistines had done to Saul, all their valiant men journeyed through the night*

to Beth Shan. They took down the bodies of Saul and his sons from the wall of Beth Shan and went to Jabot, where they burned them. Then they took their bones and buried them under a tamarisk tree at Jabot, and they fasted seven days." Could the disciple have mounted a valiant commando style raid? Where do we find them after Christ's death? From Gethsemane, they fled. Matt 26:56 *"Then all the disciples deserted him and fled".* John tells us *"On the evening of that first day of the week - the disciples were together, with the doors locked for fear of the Jews"* John 19:20. These were defeated men; they could not face the guards, because of fear.

Only the women in their devotion were brave enough to go on the first Easter morning. Their problem was not the guards but the removal of the stone, a stone so large that 4 or 5 women could not move it. Jesus certainly could not have moved it and the guards would not dare. Yet when they arrive the stone is already rolled away and the guards have fled in terror.

There is no other reasonable explanation. The body was not there because Jesus had risen from the dead, just as he promised. If the disciples did have the body, we can be sure that they would have worshipped it, as people today worship the Turin shroud, or worship at the place of Christ's birth, in the Church of the nativity.

As a young boy of twelve I remember visiting Westminster

Abbey and St Paul's Cathedral as part of a school trip. Towards the front on one side was a large glass case, and round the case several women knelt praying. I did not understand what the focus of their prayer was, until I asked, and was informed that in the case were several Holy relics. These were the focus of the misguided prayers. Throughout the medieval period, relics (the bones of saints or holy objects) were collected, which were believed to posses special powers. There have been several heads of John the Baptist, and fragments of the true cross. In Italy at the Cathedral of Monza the Iron Crown is housed, which men believe was formed around one of the nails used at the crucifixion. There has never been a relic connected to Jesus, the very thought would be blasphemy. The founder of the Christian faith is not a dead martyr but a living saviour. The Hymn writer puts it this way, *"I serve a risen Saviour, he's in the world today."* Christ not only lives in Heaven as our advocate, but by his Spirit he can dwell in the believer's heart.

A young preacher was delivering his message to a large congregation, and among his hearers was a confirmed atheist; who wrote a note and passed it to the preacher hand to hand through the congregation. The preacher stopped and read the note. It asked "what does your religion have that all these others do not have?" then listed many other religions. The Preacher wrote his reply, it read, "an empty tomb!"

5, **What else could change these timid disciples** into

fearless preachers and defenders of the resurrection? They were powerless and lost till they saw Jesus. Once they saw Jesus their courage returned; once he ascended and poured out the Holy Spirit they were unshakeable. They had seen Jesus die and now they had seen him alive. He defeated death then for 40 days proved that he was alive by appearing to those he had chosen. 1Cor 15:5-7 *"he appeared to Peter, and then to the Twelve. After that, he appeared to more than five hundred of the brothers at the same time, most of whom are still living, though some have fallen asleep. Then he appeared to James, then to all the apostles."* If the disciples had made up the story would they have been willing to face their death as martyrs for a lie? The idea that these holy men deceived people and then died for this deception is utterly preposterous. They were convinced that they had seen the risen Lord.

The Significance of the resurrection.

Firstly, the reason He appeared to followers and not to the world, is that He was calling them to be a people of faith. This was a new kind of faith. They already had faith in Jesus as the Messiah, they had followed him for three years, and they were convinced. Now they needed faith in the resurrected Christ, a man fitted for heaven, no longer confined to the limitations of this world. He makes the same call today. We are to have faith in the one who conquered death and now lives *"in the power of an indestructible life"*. (Heb 7:16.) If Christ had remained physically upon the earth, he would have been limited by both time and geography. He would have been limited in the amount of people he could see or help. Now through his resurrection he may answer the prayers of all who call upon his name. No longer limited to a physical body, he has a resurrection body.

Secondly, it proves that death is not the end. Jesus is the *"first fruits"* 1Cor 15:20 of those who will be resurrected. As the early harvest of first fruits was taken to the Temple in thanks for what would follow, so Jesus was raised the first of a mighty harvest of resurrected people. As Christ was raised, we will be raised. The Christian hope follows the same pattern as Christ: death, rest and resurrection. In the meantime we will dwell with him in paradise awaiting the resurrection morning. Luke 23:43, Eccl 12:7 *"the dust returns to the ground it came from, and the spirit returns to God who gave it."* To be in the presence of Christ for us will be heaven, but this is not the final state, we follow the same pattern as Jesus. Our body dies; it rests in the grave while our spirit enters paradise; then comes the final resurrection, when body and spirit will be reunited, and fitted for God's heavenly Kingdom.

Thirdly, it proclaims our sins are forgiven. If Christ was the lamb of God who takes away the sins of the world, it was only when he rose triumphant over the grave that we knew his offering was acceptable to God. *1Cor 15:17 +20 "If Christ has not been raised, your faith is futile; you are still in your sins.*

But Christ has indeed been raised from the dead." Christ is a living Saviour who can forgive sin and grant eternal life to all who come to him in faith. His offering was accepted and God raised him from the dead

Fourthly, this means that the message of the Scriptures and the Apostles can be trusted. This message of the resurrected Christ, forgiving all who come to him in faith, became the chief message of the Christian Church. Luke proclaims, that "t*he Christ would suffer and rise from the dead on the third day, and repentance and forgiveness of sins will be preached in his name".* Luke 24:46-47. Peter preaching to the crowd on the day of Pentecost, a mere 50 days after the Crucifixion said, *"it was impossible for death to hold him".* Festus thought Paul's message was *"about a dead man called Jesus whom Paul claimed was alive"* Acts 2:24. In the Revelation, Jesus introduces himself as *"the Living one; I was dead and behold I am alive for ever."* Rev 1:18.

Without the resurrection Christianity has no special claim to be the way to God. It is a religion no better than any other and may actually be deceiving people, based on the fantasies of people who thought they saw a dead man come back to life. But the Apostles were eye witnesses, they knew what they had seen, and left a record for us so that we should also believe. (John 20:31)

Peter said *"God raised him from the dead, freeing him from the* agony of death, because it was impossible for death to keep its hold on him." *(Acts 2:24)* The disciples of Jesus followed the man who destroyed death. This was their message; it is the still our message today.

Jesus resurrection provides the one and only safe path to God. All he taught and all He did were proved genuine by his resurrection. If this is not true, then all his other claims are to be doubted; but if he has conquered death as he promised, we must worship him as God. The Christian must learn of him today, and tomorrow share in his resurrection, in the power of his indestructible life.

"We believe that Jesus died and rose again and so we believe that God will bring with Jesus those who have fallen asleep in him. According to the Lord's own word, we tell you that we who are still alive, who are left till the coming of the Lord, will certainly not precede those who have fallen asleep. The Lord himself will come down from heaven, with a loud command, with the voice of the archangel and with the trumpet call of God, and the dead in Christ will rise first. After that, --- will be caught up together with them in the clouds to meet the Lord in the air. And so we will be with the Lord for ever". 1Thess 4:14-17.

He who testifies to these things says, "Yes, I am coming soon." Amen. Come, Lord Jesus. Rev 22:20.

Week Six: Questions for further study.

- A selection of songs and Hymns are in the appendices p150.

- Group reading: 1Cor 15:3-26, or the resurrection morning account, p100f.

- Related reading: Revelation Ch20.

- Questions marked with an* are key questions on the passage.

You do not have to cover all the questions.

Which part of the chapter on the resurrection specially spoke to you?

1: Why do people find the idea of the resurrection so hard to believe?

2*: Could the Christian faith survive without the resurrection?

3*: Paul draws five conclusions in 1Cor 15:3-8 + 12-19 about the resurrection; how do they help us?

4*: What convinces you that Christ was really dead?

5: Could the body have been stolen? How does this help the Christian cause?

6: Why did Christ only appear to His followers and not the world?

7: What hope does the resurrection bring to Christ's followers?

8: Why does the resurrection make Christ unique?

9: Is the resurrection central to your faith and why?

10: What does the term *"first fruits from the dead"* indicate?

11: Are we waiting for the undertaker or the upper taker?

12: In 1Thess 4:14f we meet those who have fallen asleep, who are they and where are they?

13: What would make our witness more confident and bold?

14: What is our hope for the future based on?

15: What was Peter's message on the day of Pentecost? Acts 2

A Prayer.

Thank you Father that faith is not based on our changeable emotions but on the resurrection of our Lord Jesus Christ. His resurrection was predicted by the Prophets, recorded in the Scriptures and proclaimed from the tomb. Thank you that men's scheming could not defeat your purposes and that you are still calling disciples today: men and women of faith, who follow on in the great cloud of witnesses knowing the power of the risen Son. May His blood cleanse us, His Spirit empower us, His wisdom guide us and His purposes be fulfilled in our lives. Keep us from hiding our faith, that we too may be witnesses of the glorious resurrection of Jesus. We do not live in the tomb but in the wonderful light of the risen Son of God. May His name be praised forever; Amen and Amen.

Memory verse week Six: - *1 Corinthians 15:20-21* **"Now is Christ risen from the dead, and become the firstfruits of them that slept. For since by man came death, by man came also the resurrection of the dead.** *KJV*

Action point: -

- Who can you invite to worship this weekend?
- Do you know of a bereaved person who needs love and support?

- Read 1Cor 15, 1Thess 4:14f, Rev 20-22 then give thanks.

Activity for the whole church: -

(You will need to prepare sticky-back hearts or put double-sided tape in the cross)

- Make enough paper hearts for the whole congregation; they may be in many colours. Ask people to write down their sins, faults and failures, or to write their own thank you prayer. Then during a hymn or in silence take the hearts and stick them to the cross.

- **Reading: Acts 2:24 + 37-38.** *'But God raised him from the dead, freeing him from the agony of death, because it was impossible for death to keep its hold on him. When the people heard this, they were cut to the heart and said to Peter and the other apostles, "Brothers, what shall we do?" Peter replied, "Repent and be baptised, every one of you, in the name of Jesus Christ for the forgiveness of sins and you will receive the gift of the Holy Spirit.'*

Through the life of Jesus in chronological order.

(A lent & Easter Bible reading plan)

If possible set aside enough time to follow each reading with reflection & prayer, talking to God about the issues raised in the reading. 15 minuets will be sufficient for most days.

Ash Wednesday: Jn1:1-18, Mt1 In John's Gospel we begin by looking at the eternal ancestry of Christ. When time itself began He was there as the express word of God to all his creation. Then in due time He entered the world to bring a fallen creation back to God, faith not ancestry was the only criteria He sought (Jn1:12). Matthew chooses to follow the human ancestry of Christ through King David's line to prove that Jesus was the true king that the nation of Israel expected: "Great David's Greater Son". He comes with a purpose, which Matthew defines, *"He will save his people from their sins."*

Thursday: Luke 1 Luke introduces his account not as an eye witness but as a historian. He gives us the background to Christ's birth, sharing stories -probably gleaned from Mary herself- that are only found in his gospel. His aim is to give a historically and accurate account of the life of Jesus. Luke is saying to his friend Theophilus, this is a true account of the life of Jesus which has been carefully researched and is based on eye witness accounts. Peter made the same claim, 2Peter 1:16.

Friday: Luke 2, Matthew 2 Luke and Matthew record all we know about Christmas. Luke carefully dates this great event, vv1-2. He tells us the first visitors were shepherds, and gives us the only insight into the early years of Jesus. The wise men in Matthew are best seen as Philosophers, Mystics or sages; they visit Bethlehem later, once the family have found a house when some of the visitors have gone home.

Saturday: Luke 3, Matthew 3 John the Baptist was the last of the Old Testament Prophets. His message was: repent and place your faith in the coming Messiah; only repentance can prepare the heart for the Lord. Baptism showed that repentance. He had been told to expect the Messiah and given a sign by which he would recognise Him. The presence of the Holy Spirit was the authentic mark of Christ's anointing. Luke again dates these events, but more importantly, Jesus is equipped for His ministry. If He needed the Holy Spirit, how much do we?

Sunday: Mark 1:1-28 Jn 1:19-51 We continue with the testimony of John the Baptist, a man of great popularity and great humility. His whole purpose was to point to Jesus the Lamb of God. Wanting to rush on to the life of Christ, Mark only gives a brief account of John's ministry. John is neither the

Messiah, nor the Groom; he is the groom's man, the best man, who prepares the way for the groom.

Mon: Matt 4 1-17, Lk 4:1-30 Jn 2:1-11 The first thing the Spirit does is to take Jesus into a head on conflict with Satan. The Spirit's guidance is not always easy. Luke and Matthew have a different order of events; it is probable that Luke is making a chronological record but Matthew is making a theological point by having Satan offer the Kingdom last.

Tue: Jn 2:12-Jn 3:21 + Jn 4 Mk 1:29-34 Lk 4:31-44. Jesus first preaching tour of Galilee ends with a trip to the Passover at Jerusalem. John alone describes this trip, the first cleansing of the temple, the meeting with Nicodemus and the trip back to Galilee. On the way He meets the Samaritan woman. For her and Nicodemus the issue is a living faith versus a dead religion. We must be born again; this is not a religious phrase but a vital experience, a spiritual rebirth through faith in Christ. We must receive the Spirit for only then can we worship as God intends. From the start Jesus knew He was destined to die and rise again; in the cleansing of the temple He makes this the proof of His ministry.

Wed: Lk 5 to 6:16, Matt 4:18-25 The Apostles are called. It seems that at first the disciples only followed Jesus in their spare time. They had met Him with John the Baptist at the

Jordan, and seen His miracles, now it is time for them to decide. Simon Peter sees clearly his own sin as an obstacle to following Christ. In Christ's holy presence he is aware of his unholy nature. Until we face our own sin we can never face an almighty God.

Thurs: Mt 5+6 The sermon on the mount was specifically given to Jesus' disciples, it is not about salvation, but shows the standard of life which God expects to develop in His followers. The beatitudes focus on our great need and God's great supply. God calls not those who have spiritual strength, but those who are spiritually weak, those who are poor in spirit. Here is a ladder which measures our spiritual growth; poverty of spirit, mourning for sin, meekness, hunger for God, mercy, purity etc.

Fri: Matt 7+8:1-22 The sermon continues presenting a Christian's life style. We must judge ourselves first, and then we can help others. We must continue in persevering prayer, we must build a life on the teachings of Christ, if we want it to stand the tests of this life and the next. Christ's teachings amaze the people as they recognised His authority. In chapter 8 we find people's responses to Christ's authority. They come with a certainty of faith that Christ can heal them.

Sat: Lk 6:17 to 7:50. As Jesus resumes His preaching tour He delivers the sermon on the plain, a follow-up to the Sermon on the Mount, this is not the same as Matthew's account but again concentrating on the character of a true disciple. It was by repetition that Jesus taught His disciples. Both sinners and Pharisees seek Him out. How do we view ourselves? Greatly forgiven and loving much, or do we think our sins are little? The result will be that we only love Christ a little. Whether our sins are obvious or hidden, they still offend God greatly. Too often church members think they are not sinners. It is only when we face our sin that we really have a testimony of Christ's forgiveness. Remember sin can be in thought, word and deed.

Sun: Mk 4, Lk 8, Mt 8:23-34. The storm, the swine and the demon possessed man are in all three synoptic Gospels. It seems there were actually 2 men. Mk 7 and Lk 8 concentrate on the one who wanted to follow Jesus. The superstitious residents, not Israelites, are afraid of Jesus who has more power than this man with evil spirits. When Jesus sends him home, he finds his job is not to be an Apostle but a witness. His story prepares the way for Jesus' next visit, when many respond.

Mon: Mk 5:1-6:13 Jesus through the Holy Spirit carried the tangible anointing of God (the Christ means the anointed one). He felt power go out from him when the woman with constant bleeding touched Him. Christ carried the anointing, but it was released by the touch of faith. He also passed that anointing and power to His disciples when they went out to preach. It is the touch of faith that will release His power today.

Tue: Lk 9:1-9, Mt 10. Jesus speaks to His disciples as they go out on their mission. His warning is that some will accept and some reject them. Whenever a Christian is rejected then Christ Himself is rejected. The same principle applies today, when people reject Christ's followers, they are rejecting Christ. Christ's message can either save or bring judgement; this division can even come within a family!

Wed: Jn 3:22-36, Mt 11. John the Baptist had seen clearly that Christ's ministry must grow and his come to an end. He was the best man not the groom, but facing death in prison brought a severe test to his faith. Jesus said John was the greatest of Old Testament prophets, yet the simplest Christian has a greater standing than John, because he sees the full light of God's kingdom; in Jesus, he stands under the dispensation of grace, not merely at the door. Christ was building His Church; believers were being called sons, not servants. Those who repented under John, were now entering into strong assurance of faith, those who rejected were now becoming hardened.

Thurs: Mt 12+13, Jn 5. Jesus confronted hypocrisy head on, but the people, He taught in parables. The parable gave them both a story to remember and a deeper meaning to ponder upon. Parables have a hidden meaning; they can be dismissed as children's stories or received as keys to the kingdom. The parables are uncompromising and give an insight into what Jesus himself felt was deeply important. At the end of this time He returns to Jerusalem again where the man by the pool is healed.

Fri: Mk 6:14-29, Mt 14:1-12. Sin caused the adulterous wife of Herod to hate John. (Sin hates to be discovered.) Lust caused Herod to offer the daughter of Herodias a kingdom, an easily led youth requested the prophet's head, and pride ordered his murder. Jesus, in sorrow for his cousin and distressed at man's wickedness, retires to the wilderness.

Sat: Mk 6:30-43, Mt 14 13-21. The feeding of the 5,000 is the only miracle, except for the resurrection, which appears in all 4 gospels. Jesus tired and grieving as He is still, has compassion on the crowds. His aim was solitude but the father made other arrangements. How do we respond when our plans are suddenly changed? Do we see God's hand guiding us or are we resentful of the time which is stolen?

Sun: Lk 9 10-17, Jn 6 1:25. Luke tells us that Jesus had been teaching the crowds before He fed them. John says this combination of teaching and miracles caused them to want to make Him king by force. Jesus steps back from this mass acclaim, and hides Himself from the crowd in prayer. His aim is always God's will not man's approval. Popularity can be a snare; our goal is to please God whatever men say.

Mon: Mk 6:45-56, Mt 14:22-36 Once the disciples are alone, Satan takes the opportunity to try and destroy them in a storm. It is often when we are alone, that the enemy will seek to destroy our faith. Out of the storm comes Jesus. With his eyes on Jesus, Peter stretches his faith and walks on the water. When he takes his eyes from Christ, he wavers and sinks. Do not be too hard on Peter, all the others stayed in the boat. The end result is an absolute conviction of the authority of Jesus.

Tue: Jn 6:25-70 + Jn 7. John is the only one who shows the full reason for the miracle of feeding of the 5,000. It is to show that Jesus is the bread of heaven; that a man may eat and never die. A heated argument follows about eternal life and how to be saved. Jesus is very clear: only faith, in the one God has sent, can bring a person to salvation. After further travels Jesus goes to the feast of tabernacles. This feast lasts a week; it is held in September at the beginning of the Jewish New Year. It is similar to our harvest festival, but the Jews dwelt in booths (tents) to remember the wilderness wanderings.

Wed: Jn 8+9. Jesus stays in Jerusalem after the feast; two important stories are told here. Some early manuscripts miss out the woman caught in adultery. Why? Could it be seen as too sensitive, with Jesus condoning sin? The received text, which the King James Version uses, has the story; the versions used by many modern translators do not. Which text is better is a value judgement. The story shows Jesus not condoning sin but forgiving it; the woman is expected to change. "Go and sin no more", this is the message to us too. In the next chapter Jesus heals physical blindness but cannot heal stubborn spiritual blindness.

Thurs: Jn 10:1-21, Mk 7. In these chapters, Jesus offers life to the Pharisees. In John, we have two of his important "I AM" sayings. The Pharisees could not progress beyond religious laws. They could not see that a loving response of faith mattered more than rules. This kind of believer still abounds "following the traditions of men" rather than the love of God. We must take care not to fall into this trap. Remember "People matter more than things". Jesus was able to go beyond man made laws when He delivered the daughter of the Syrophenician woman. Her faith saved her daughter, and the law was powerless to prevent it.

Fri: Mt 15, Mk 8. Cleanness of heart is not found in what we do but in who we are. Jesus did not only feed 5,000. He also fed another 4,000. Even after this the Pharisees wanted a sign from heaven. This is stubborn unbelief. Yet to those who will believe, more is given: a blind man is healed and Peter receives a profound revelation of who Christ is.

Sat: Mt 16, Lk 9:18-27. Jesus is now at the height of His popularity and the opposition of the Pharisees is growing. He now asks the disciples to speak of their faith (cf Rom 10:9-10) and reveals that the whole purpose of the coming of the Christ is that He may die. As is often the case, we must put the three gospels together to get the full picture of the confession which Peter made. "You are the Christ, the Son of the living God."

Sun: Matt 17:1-13, Mk 9:1-13, Lk 9:28-36. The Transfiguration is one of the most glorious points in the ministry of Christ; heaven and earth seem to merge into one. Moses and Elijah are allowed to stand with Jesus and speak of his Exodus (death) at Jerusalem. The word is chosen carefully; it refers back to the first covenant made at the Exodus from Egypt, and shows that Christ will by His death / exodus make a New Covenant. On the mountain the essence of Deity, Jesus true Godhead, shines briefly for all to see. For one moment on earth He is the Eternal Christ again. Peter never forgot this day, see 2 Peter 1:16 - 23. The presence of His glory will indelibly change all who witness it.

Mon: Mt 17:14-27, Mk 9:14-50, Lk 9:37-50. From now on Jesus is heading steadily toward His final conflict in Jerusalem. The disciples seem powerless without Christ's presence; their lack of power reveals a lack of prayer and even of fasting, says Matthew. Since he was one who had little faith, he should know. Their eyes seem to be on their own prestige not on Christ's coming death. We all tend to be more preoccupied with ourselves. This is inappropriate in the presence of Christ. For every one look at our hearts, we should take ten at Christ; only then will we have the right balance of life and a strong faith.

Tue: Luke 9:51-10:41. On His way to Jerusalem, Jesus is still concerned to send out the message of the kingdom of God. Samaritans resist His message, others make excuses. Jesus is not put off; He speaks plainly *"you proclaim the kingdom of God"*. He even sends out 72 others to proclaim the message. If they are accepted Christ is accepted; if they are rejected, Christ is turned away. Whether people listen or not it is still our duty to speak both *"in season and out of season"* 2Tim 4:2. He finally arrives at Bethany, two miles from Jerusalem, where his friend Lazarus, Martha and Mary live.

Wed: Jn 10:22-38, Lk 11+12 Jesus may have been going to Jerusalem for the feast of dedication (Hanukkah), held about the time of our Christmas which celebrates the rebuilding of the temple under Judas Maccabees (See book of Maccabees, the Apocrypha). In Luke 11+12 we have some of Jesus' sermons as He taught His disciples and preached to the crowds, warning them they did not understand the momentous days they were living in. Many today do not see the signs of the times!

Thur: Lk 13+14. Repentance and holiness are the key notes of Luke 13+14. God judges us not by how we appear but by how we truly are. He looks for fruit of character and conduct, He knows the road we walk on is narrow, but it leads to the broad uplands of eternity. Cf Isaiah 35:8-10. The broad road proclaims freedom but truly leads to death.

Fri: Lk 15, Mt 18. Luke alone gives us these three parables of Jesus. They represent types of people that He came to seek and to save. The sheep was foolishly lost, the coin did not know it was lost, the son was stubbornly lost. He sought and welcomed back each one. Yet Matthew tells us not only to seek the lost but to seek to be at one with any who sin against us. We are to be forgiving because we have been forgiven.

Sat: Lk 16 + 17 + 18:1-7. These parables contain weighty and famous sayings: 1, we cannot serve two masters. 2, our Lord's attitude to divorce is different to the world's. 3, someone rising from the dead will not even convince some people of the reality of Heaven and Hell. When we feel unjustly treated we must remember we are but servants. God's kingdom is a hidden reality which will one day be openly revealed, and until then we must persevere and pray as Jesus himself did.

Passion Sun: Mt 19:1-15, Mk 10:1-16. Here Jesus clarifies His teaching on divorce; while it is not right for any and every reason, adultery severs the marriage bond. Marriage is the exclusive union of one man and one woman for life. It is publicly acknowledged in the wedding ceremony, permanently sealed by both God and the couple as they take their vows, and physically consummated in the act of sexual union. In marriage we covenant to each other, to leave behind our past, cleave to each other in a new relationship and through physical union become one flesh. It is interesting that following this discussion the children are blessed. Outside marriage we miss out on God's blessing.

Mon: Mt 19:16-20:16, Mk 10:17-31, Lk 18:18-30. The young man comes with a good question, he is seeking salvation. The account shows clearly that salvation is an act of God, and not due to our obedience. The commandment Jesus avoids mentioning: is you shall not covet. The problem he needed to face was his covetousness, he had to face himself. We cannot follow Christ and expect to stay the same. Matthew sets our responsibility to repent against God's grace when we do.

Tue: John 10:40 +11. It is during this time that Jesus is staying across the Jordan (Matt 19:1 + Jn 10:40-41) That he is called back to raise Lazarus is from the dead. It is this single miracle more than anything else that causes the rulers to decide to kill Him; the very miracle which proved His claim to be Lord of life and death. The key verse is Jn 11:25. The raising of Lazarus is the proof that Jesus would fulfil His word and return from the grave. Some people say that they will believe in life after death when someone comes back to prove it, the truth is they will never believe, this is an excuse, since they do not believe in Jesus the One who returned from the dead.

Wed: Mt 20:17-34, Mk 10:32-52, Lk 18:31-43 Each Gospel

writer continues with Jesus telling us that our salvation, will be through His death, not by keeping the commandments, but the disciples do not yet understand. They are still centred on their own position and prestige. God needs to deal with our selfishness and pride. James and John enlist their mother's help and come to Jesus seeking the highest places in His kingdom. This He could not grant, but He did reveal that God will mature and develop us, through suffering. Christ suffered for speaking the truth, (CF Jn 18:23) Paul also says that suffering may be our path to maturity. (Phil 3:11) Conversely Bartimaeus who seeks no glory is freed from suffering.

Thurs: Lk 19:1-28, Jn 12:1-11, Mk 14:1-9. Jesus is now near Jerusalem; we are entering the last week of his life on earth. He passes through Jericho, where Zacchaeus seeks and finds the saviour. He then moves on to Bethany, lodging with Martha, Lazarus and Mary. This is a difficult portion of the Bible. The dates seem all wrong. How do we reconcile these accounts? We read what it actually says! Jesus came to Bethany six days before the Passover (Saturday). From there He taught and preached to the crowds, travelling to Jerusalem each day. The Feast and anointing of Jesus were not held at the house of Lazarus, on the night of His arrival but at Simon the Leper's a few days later on Wednesday only two days before the feast of Passover being Friday. Most of the writers hide the woman's identity, since she was known to be immoral, but here we find a testimony of grace, Jesus came to seek and to save the lost. John tells us she is now a disciple, Mary the sister of Martha and Lazarus. We do not need to parade our past, but neither do we need to feel it will keep us from following Christ.

Fri: Mt 21:1-17, Jn 12:12-50 The Triumphal entry really boils the pot. The crowds think Jesus has come to save them and He has. They shout Hosanna, "Lord save us", but they don't know the cost of their salvation. The rulers continue in unbelief, and Greeks for the first time ask to see Jesus. The Gospel is about to be opened to the nations and the seed must be planted. The desire of the Greeks was good. May it be our desire also: "We would see Jesus." Roy Hessian's book, "We would see Jesus", is a classic in and well worth reading. Pub Rickfords Hill Publishing £1 Classics. Also on CLC.

Sat: Lk 19:28-47, Mk 11. Following the triumphal entry, Jesus again cleanses the Temple (cf Jn2:12.for the first occasion.) The first time He told them the Temple was not a market place; this time He tells them it is a House of Prayer for all nations. Mark alone gives us the date of the cleansing of the temple. It was not on the Sunday following His entry into Jerusalem, but on the Monday morning, the same day that He welcomed the children, healed the sick and taught the people. The cursing of the fig tree is a parable of the barrenness of the nation of Israel. Though they saw so many miracles, and heard Christ gladly, they did not produce the fruit of repentance.

Palm Sun: Mt 21:20-46, Mk 11:20-12:40, Lk 20. It is now Tuesday of Holy Week, the authorities are seeking to challenge Jesus. Since they did not accept John the Baptist, Christ's forerunner, how could they accept the Christ? Jesus' question shows up their indecision, and His parables begin to focus on their unbelief. The son who says he will obey and does not is the unbelieving Jew; the son who says he will not and does finally obey, is the believing Gentile. Christ Himself is the son of the vineyard owner, whom the tenants reject and kill, but in rejecting the son they lose their inheritance.

Mon: Mt 23, Mk 12:41-44, Lk 21:1-5. We rarely see Jesus angry, but here His anger at the stubborn unbelief of the leaders bursts over their heads. Matthew alone records the seven woes against the scribes and Pharisees. Their religion has becomes an obstacle to their seeing God. This must be a warning to us; they "strain at a gnat and swallow a camel". Religion alone, ceremony and law, can never bring us into God's kingdom. Man can only enter God's kingdom when he is made righteous, and Christian righteousness is different from all other kinds of righteousness. There is civil or political righteousness, which nations and governments deal with. There is right living before our fellow men, a matter of correct manners and actions. There is the righteousness the Pharisees sought, by obeying the commandments, which clearly did not work, and there is righteousness through faith (Rom 1:17) this is Christian righteousness. (See Martin Luther's commentary on Galatians.) Jesus was more impressed with the faith of a humble widow, than the outward righteousness of the rulers.

Tue: Mt 24, Mk 13, Lk 21:5-38. Jesus is probably leaving the Temple, through what we now call Warren's gate, in the western facing wall of the temple. There the largest stones still sit, some weighing over 100 tonnes. The disciples marvel, while Jesus looks from the glory of man to the glory of God. Man's kingdoms will fall; God's will stand forever. Here, we are given specific information about the return of Christ and His coming kingdom.   Here, we hear of the "great tribulation." When interpreting prophecy we should bear in mind two things: 1, setting specific times is discouraged by Jesus; 2, in these passages He begins by speaking directly to His disciples and then broadens out to the signs of the end of the age. We may find four ages in the scripture: 1, the age of innocence; 2, the age of the Law; 3, the age of grace; 4, the kingdom of God. Our calling is not to speculate but to be watchful.

Wed: Mt 25:1 - 26:16, Mk 14:1-10, Lk 22:7-53. Having spoken of the certainty of the Kingdom of heaven, Jesus now tells His disciples throughout history to be ready for its appearing. These are His last parables: the ten virgins, the talents, and the sheep and the goats; all have one central message. The kingdom will not appear at once; Christ's followers must: 1, be ready whenever He returns; 2, serve Him diligently by using their gifts to His glory; 3, show their faith by their works. The "sheep and the goats" is not a simple plea for good works, but a warning that our works must match our words. If we claim to be sheep but are not committed to Christ or His people, we will face His judgement not His approval, for some this will be a great shock.

Maundy Thurs: Jn 13:1-17, Mk 14:12-31, Jn 14-15-16, Lk 22:47-53. So much happened at the last supper that we cannot cover it all. It began with Christ humbling Himself to wash the disciples' feet, it continued with Judas going out into the night, the man of darkness, given over to darkness. Peter's betrayal is predicted and the new covenant meal is established. In the Bible often a covenant has a sign to show those who are included in its benefits. Noah's covenant had a rainbow, Moses' covenant was sealed with circumcision, the New covenant, in Christ's blood, was given the sign of bread and wine, to bring to mind the great cost of our cleansing and forgiveness. Then finally Christ taught His disciples to expect the Holy Spirit, who would be their comforter, strength and guide. After His prayer Jn 17, He is then arrested and taken to the High Priest.

Good Fri: Mt 27:1-10, Jn 18:1 – 19:37, Lk 23: 6-46. The motive of Judas in handing Jesus over is unclear; it may have been jealousy, greed or disillusion. The sadness is that he did not live past the crucifixion and resurrection. Had he seen the risen Christ, he too may have found repentance unto life. Pilate was known as a brutal dictator, yet he fears the Jews. First he tries to pass the buck, then he declares Jesus innocent, finally he gives way to the persistent demands of the crowd, releases a criminal, and seeks to absolve himself by washing his hands. It was not only the hatred of the Jewish leaders, but also Pilate's weakness that put Jesus on the cross. *"A man's heart plans his way, but the LORD directs his steps" Prov 16:9.* Christ died in the purpose and foreknowledge of God.

Holy Sat: Mt 27:45-66, Lk 23:50-56, Jn 19:32-42. On that day of waiting nothing but the cross would be in the minds of the disciples. Their doors were locked, their hearts were cold, and their hope was gone; Jesus was in the tomb. Joseph had bravely gone to Pilate in defiance of his own people and fulfilled scripture by burying Christ in a rich man's tomb (Isaiah 53:9). The centurion had confirmed His death with the spear thrust to the heart, and then Joseph had embalmed the body. What they could not know was at that very moment Christ was proclaiming His victory to the world of the dead and liberating all the faithful from Abraham's bosom. (1 Pet 3:19, Lk 16:19-31)

Easter Sun: Jn 20:1-23, Mt 28:1-15, Mk 16:1-8, Lk 24:1-35. The women rose early on that first day of the week, but

Christ rose earlier. Five groups of witnesses saw Him on that first Lord's Day: Mary Magdalene; the women returning from the tomb; Simon Peter, who kept secret what Christ said to him; the men going to Emmaus; and the ten in the upper room. *"Look yea saints the sight is glorious, see the man of sorrows now. From the fight return victorious, every knee to him must bow, crown him crown him, crowns become the victor's brow."*

Easter Monday: Lk 24:36-49, John 20:24 - 21:25. On the resurrection morning Thomas was not present. It was a week later that Jesus appeared to him and doubting Thomas believed in the resurrection. Thomas makes the true Christian confession: that Jesus is both Lord and God. John tells us more, he tells of the restoration of Peter and of the purpose of the gospels that all may believe. Hearing the story of Christ is not meant to educate or entertain us, it is meant to bring us to a living faith. Jn 21:31. Christians may approach the Father, through the Son, in the power of the Holy Spirit. Matthew 28 has the first Trinitarian formula used by Christ himself.

Tues after Easter: Mt 28:16-20, Mk 16:9-20, Lk 24:50-53, Acts 1:1-11. Our last reading takes us to the ascension. Christ left His followers with a mission to spread the message of forgiveness through faith in His death. People have argued that the end of Mark's gospel is a later addition. However if it is, it only proves that the power which Christ bestowed at Pentecost continued in the Church down the years. There would be no need to add words about miracles if they had ceased with the ascension. As Jesus left, He lifted His hands in blessing, His hands are still lifted in blessing today, and we have the promise of angels that He will return, in the same way that He went. We look for the clouds to part and Christ's eternal reign to begin. If you wish to follow what happened next, then continue reading the book of Acts as Christ's Apostles establish the infant Church.

Appendix 1: The Centurion's Story: wk 5
A monologue on Christ's Passion,
Matthew 27:54 & John 19:35.

It is strange what money does to a man. A powerful pull, is the lust for money, souls are bought for a bag of gold. I'm a Centurion, 100 men are under my command and this bag of money is the price of a house to me. Yes! I was on duty during Passover. We all were, these Jewish religious feasts can end in trouble, and this year they were excited about a Prophet from Galilee. You should have heard the din last Sunday as he rode into town. The crowds were cheering about the return of David's Kingdom; they threw their clothes before him, danced and sung. "Blessed is the coming kingdom of our father David. Hosanna, save us" they shouted. Some said he was the "Son of God" but when he came past he was riding a donkey.

The next morning, there were screams from the temple; the Prophet was whipping the money changers. We could see it from the fortress. People scattered everywhere. The temple guards sent to arrest him could only say, "No man ever spoke like this one." They just left him teaching the crowds.

It was early on Friday that I woke. I hadn't slept well; people were milling about in the courtyard. They had lit a fire and when the cock crowed I just wanted to get back to sleep, but it crowed again and I knew the day beckoned. I could have throttled the bird when it crowed a third time, but I swear as I stumbled out of bed, I could hear a man sobbing by the barrack room wall.

Then the call came to attend on Pilate. There was a crowd before the judgement seat. They were surly and angry, pushing and jostling. The Prophet stood silently before them with a purple robe and a crown of thorns pinned to his head. The lectors had already whipped him, and as Pilate stepped forward I remember his words, "Behold the Man!" "No God here", Pilate was saying; and a wave of hatred rolled forward from the crowd, - how could they love him on Sunday and hate him on Friday? You could feel the air bristle with an intense loathing, centring on this Jesus. We could barely hold them back. A small group of women cried for his release, but not a man to be seen. "What shall I do with your king?" asked Pilate. "Crucify Him" they bawled. The mob was uncontrollable. Then Pilate took a bowl washed his hands and gave them Jesus.

Seven times he spoke on the cross, I heard every word. As the nails pierced his hand he prayed, "Father forgive them they do not know what they are doing." The two thieves crucified with him were swearing and cursing him, till one of them changed his mind. He said, "Lord, remember me when you come into your kingdom" and Jesus promised him paradise. It was when the darkness came that Jesus panicked, - it was a thick sad darkness, as darkness you could feel, - and looking round he cried "My Father, why have you abandoned me?"

Three hours the darkness lasted, from noon till three, then he lifted his head, cried loudly: "it is finished" and lowering his head whispered, "Father into your hands I commit my Spirit." That was when I spoke. It seemed obvious, it came from somewhere within me, I hardly knew I was speaking as the word's formed: "Truly," I said, "This man was the Son of God." They buried him in a rich man's tomb; my boys were given guard duty. Now that's a first, guarding a tomb; a real live bunch they are down there. I slept back at the barracks.

Then this morning, Sunday, I was called to the High Priest's house, which is very unusual; they really don't like having Romans in their houses, these Jewish leaders. It turns out that the body was missing. My boys had fallen asleep! "Dereliction of duty", I said; I was off to call the Governor and have them flogged. Take the complaint seriously I thought; they will like that! "No need to be hasty", said Caiaphas. "Take this money", he said; each of us received a bag of gold, all the guards and me! "If anyone asks, say his disciples stole the body while you slept, and we satisfy the governor". That was the story.

All I need to do is say that: "He was dead". Well I knew that, I had seen the spear in his side, I had seen the water and the blood; so why doesn't this pay off seem right? Then I heard that some women claimed they had seen him alive. They said, "He is not here, He has risen!" What about the money? (He drops the Money bag) I think I need to speak to one of His followers; John; that was his name!

Appendix 2:
The Passion account set in 6 voices
(From Matthew, Mark, Luke & John.)

Cast: - Narrator, Jesus, Crowd/Congregation; more than one voice, Soldier, Criminals 1 & 2.

(May be read on either week one or week five.)

Narrator: Carrying his own cross, he went out to the place of the Skull (which in Aramaic is called Golgotha). There they crucified him, along with the criminals-- one on his right, the other on his left. Jesus said,

Jesus; **"Father, forgive them, for they do not know what they are doing."**

Narrator: Pilate had a notice prepared and fastened to the cross. It read: JESUS OF NAZARETH, THE KING OF THE JEWS. Many of the Jews read this sign, for the place where Jesus was crucified was near the city, and the sign was written in Aramaic, Latin and Greek. The chief priests of the Jews protested to Pilate,

Crowd: "Do not write 'The King of the Jews', but that this man claimed to be king of the Jews."

Narrator: Pilate answered, "What I have written, I have written." It was the third hour when they crucified him. --- Those who passed by hurled insults at him, shaking their heads and saying,

Crowd: "So! You, who are going to destroy the temple and build it in three days, come down from the cross and save yourself!" Come down from the cross, if you are the Son of

God!"

Narrator: The soldiers - took his clothes, dividing them into four shares, one for each of them, with the undergarment remaining. This garment was seamless, woven in one piece from top to bottom they said to one another.

Soldier: "Let's not tear it; let's decide by lot who will get it."

Narrator: This happened that the scripture might be fulfilled which said, "They divided my garments among them and cast lots for my clothing."

In the same way the chief priests, the teachers of the law and the elders mocked him.

Crowd: "He saved others," they said, "but he can't save himself! He's the King of Israel! Let him come down now from the cross, and we will believe in him. He trusts in God. Let God rescue him now if he wants him, for he said, 'I am the Son of God.'"

Narrator: The soldiers also came up and mocked him. They offered him wine vinegar and said,

Soldiers: "If you are the king of the Jews, save yourself."

Narrator: Near the cross of Jesus stood his mother, his mother's sister, Mary the wife of Clopas, and Mary Magdalene. When Jesus saw his mother there, and the disciple whom he loved standing near by, he said to his mother,

Jesus: **"Dear woman, here is your son,"**

Narrator: and to the disciple,

Jesus: **"Here is your mother."**

Narrator: From that time on, this disciple took her into his home. One of the criminals who hung there hurled insults at him:

Criminal: 1 "Aren't you the Christ? Save yourself and us!"

Narrator: But the other criminal rebuked him.

Criminal 2 "Don't you fear God, since you are under the same sentence? We are punished justly, for we are getting what our deeds deserve. But this man has done nothing wrong." "Jesus, remember me when you come into your kingdom."

Jesus: "I tell you the truth, today you will be with me in paradise."

Narrator: At the sixth hour darkness came over the whole land until the ninth hour. And Jesus cried out in a loud voice, "Eloi, Eloi, lama sabachthani?"--

Jesus: "My God, my God, why have you forsaken me?"

Narrator: When some of those standing near heard this, they said,

Crowd: "Listen, he's calling Elijah."

Narrator: Knowing that all was now completed, and so that the Scripture would be fulfilled, Jesus said,

Jesus: "I am thirsty."

Narrator: A jar of wine vinegar was there; immediately one of them ran and got a sponge. He filled it with wine vinegar, put it on a stick, and offered it to Jesus to drink. The rest said,

Crowd: "Now leave him alone. Let's see if Elijah comes to save him."

Narrator: When he had received the drink, Jesus said with a loud voice,

Jesus: **"It is finished."** **"Father, into your hands I commit my spirit.**

Narrator: With that, he bowed his head and gave up his spirit. At that moment the curtain of the temple was torn in two from top to bottom. The earth shook and the rocks split. When the centurion, who stood there in front of Jesus, heard his cry and saw how he died, he said,

Soldier: "Surely this man was the Son of God!"

Appendix 3.

Easter Sunday in chronological order!

It has been argued that the events of the first Easter morning are so confused and contradictory that it is impossible to say with certainty the order of events. The following seems to me to be the order which best fits the witnesses. The only question I have not yet resolved is how many Angels the women saw. It seems there were actually several Angelic appearances: outside and inside the tomb, a separate one with Mary alone, and another with the women on the road. Some saw one angel, others saw two; each reporting what they saw. However they probably said nothing till after Mary met Jesus in the garden and encouraged by her certainty they together shared their stories.

Easter Sunday, the resurrection morning a suggested chronology:

Luke 23:55-56 The women, who came with him from Galilee, followed, and saw the sepulchre, and how his body was laid. They returned, and prepared spices and ointments; and rested on the Sabbath day according to the commandment. **Mark 16:1-3** When the Sabbath was past, Mary Magdalene, and Mary the mother of James, and Salome, bought sweet spices, that they might come and anoint him. Very early in the morning the first day of the week, they came unto the sepulchre at the rising of the sun. And said, -- Who shall roll away the stone from the door of the sepulchre?

Matt 28:2-4. There was a great earthquake: for the angel of the Lord descended from heaven, and came and rolled back the stone from the door, and sat upon it. His countenance was like lightning, and his raiment white as snow: - The guards shook, and became as dead men.

MK 16:-4-8. When the women looked, they saw that the stone was rolled away: -- And entering into the sepulchre, they saw a young man sitting on the right side, clothed in a long white garment; and they were affrighted. He said to them, be not afraid: You seek Jesus of Nazareth, which was crucified: he is risen; he is not here: behold the place where they laid him. **Luke 24:5-8.** And as they -- bowed their faces to the earth, he said, why do you seek the living among the dead? He is not here, but is risen: remember how he spoke to you when he was in Galilee, saying: "The Son of man must be delivered into the hands of sinful men, and be crucified, and the third day rise again". And they remembered his words. **Mark 16:7-8.** But go your way, tell his disciples and Peter that he is going before you into Galilee: there you shall see him, as he said unto you. And they went out quickly, and fled from the sepulchre; for they trembled and were amazed: neither said they any thing to any man; for they were afraid.

John 20:1, 3-17. Mary Magdalene – ran to Simon Peter, and to the other disciple, who Jesus loved, and said to them, they have taken away the Lord -- and we do not know where they have laid him. Peter went, with the other disciple, and came to the sepulchre. They ran together: and the other disciple outrun Peter, and arrived first. Stooping down, and looking in, (he) saw the linen clothes lying; yet he did not enter. Then Simon Peter came --and went into the sepulchre, and saw the linen clothes, and the napkin, that was about his head, not lying with the linen clothes, but wrapped - by itself. Then the other disciple went in, who had arrived first -- and he saw, and believed. As yet they did not know from the scripture, that he must rise again from the dead. Then the disciples went to their own home.

Mark 16:9 Now when Jesus arose early the first day of the week, he appeared first to Mary Magdalene, out of whom he had cast seven devils. **John 20:11-17.** Mary stood outside the sepulchre weeping: and as she wept, she stooped down, and looked in. She saw two angels in white sitting, the one at the head, and the other at the feet, where the body of Jesus had lain. And they said to her, Woman, why do you weep? She said because they have taken away my Lord, and I know not where they have laid him. And when she had said this, she turned, and saw Jesus standing, but did not know that it was Jesus. Jesus said to her, Woman, why are you weeping? Who do you seek? She, supposing him to be the gardener said, Sir, if you have carried him away, tell me where you have laid him, and I will take him away. Jesus said to her, Mary. She turned, and said, Rabboni; which is to say, Master. Jesus said to her, Touch me not; for I am not yet ascended to my Father: but go to my brethren, and say to them, I am ascending to my Father, and your Father; and to my God, and your God.

[THEN] **Matt 28:9-10.** As the women were going to tell his disciples, - Jesus met them, saying: "All hail". They came and held him by the feet, and worshipped him. Then said Jesus unto them, do not be afraid: go tell my brethren to go to Galilee, there they shall see me.

Matt 28:11-15. Now as the women were going, - some of the guards came to the city, and told the chief priests all the things that had happened. And when they were assembled with the elders, and had taken counsel, they gave large money to the soldiers, Saying, You are to say, His disciples came by night, and stole him away while we slept. And if this comes to the governor's ears, we will convince him, and rescue you. So they took the money, and did as they were told: and this saying is commonly reported among the Jews to this day.

John 20:18 Mary Magdalene came and told the disciples that she had seen the Lord, and that he had spoken these things unto her. [THE OTHER WOMEN SOON JONINED HER] **Mt 28:10** It was Mary Magdalene, and Joanna, and Mary the mother of James, and other women that were with them, which told these things unto the apostles. But their words seemed like foolish tales, and they did not believe them.

Mark 16:12 After that he appeared in another form unto two of them, as they walked, and went into the country. **Luke 26:13 – 36.** Two of them went that same day to a village called Emmaus, which was about threescore furlongs from Jerusalem. And they talked together of all these things. It came to pass, that, while they spoke together and reasoned, Jesus himself drew near, and walked with them. But their eyes were closed so that they did not know him. And he said to them, what are you talking about, hat makes you so sad? And the one of them, - named Cleopas, answered, Are you only a stranger in Jerusalem, who does not know the things which are come to pass in these days? And he said to them, what things? And they said, Concerning Jesus of Nazareth, who was a prophet mighty in deed and word before God and all the people: And how the chief priests and our rulers delivered him to be condemned to death, and have crucified him. But we trusted that he was the one to redeem Israel: and beside all this, to day is the third day since this happened, and certain of our women astonished us, --

when they did not find his body. They said that they had also seen a vision of angels, who said that he was alive. And some of us -- went to the sepulchre, and found it just as the women had said: but him they did not see.

Then he said O fools, and slow of heart to believe all that the prophets have spoken: Ought not Christ to have suffered these things, and to enter into his glory? And beginning at Moses and all the prophets, he expounded unto them in all the scriptures the things concerning himself. And as they drew near to the village, -- and he made as though he would go further. But they constrained him, saying, Abide with us: for it is almost evening, and the day is over. And he went in to stay with them. And --, as he sat at meat with them, he took bread, and blessed it, and broke, and gave to them. And their eyes were opened, and they knew him; and he vanished out of their sight. And they said one to each other; did not our heart burn within us, while he talked with us by the way, and while he opened to us the scriptures? And they rose up the same hour, and returning to Jerusalem, and found the eleven gathered together, -- Saying, The Lord is risen indeed, and hath appeared to Simon. And they told them what had happened as they walked, and how he was known to them in breaking of bread.

John 20:19, The same evening, - the first day of the week, when the doors were shut - and the disciples were assembled for fear of the Jews, Jesus came and stood in the midst, and said to them, Peace be unto you.

Mark 16:14. As they sat at the meal, He upbraided them for their unbelief and hardness of heart, because they did not believe those who had seen him after he was raised.

Luke 24:37-49 they were terrified – supposing that they had seen a spirit. And he said to them, why are ye troubled? And why do doubts arise in your hearts? Behold my hands and my feet, it is I myself: handle me, and see; for a spirit has not flesh and bones, as you see I have. And when he had spoken, he showed them his hands and his feet. And while they yet believed not for joy, and wondered, he said to them, Have you any food? And they gave him a piece of a broiled fish, and a honeycomb. He took it, and ate it before them. He said to them, these are the words which I spoke to you, while I was with you, that all things must be fulfilled, which were written in the Law of Moses, and in the prophets, and in the psalms, concerning me. Then he opened their understanding, that they might understand the scriptures, And said to them, It is written, that the Christ had to suffer, and to rise from the dead the third day: So that repentance and remission of sins should be preached in his name among all nations, beginning at Jerusalem. And ye are witnesses of these things. Behold, I send the promise of my Father upon you: but wait in the city of

Jerusalem, until you are endued with power from on high.

John 20: 20 - 29 and --he showed them his hands and his side. Then the disciples were glad, when they saw the Lord. Jesus said to them-, Peace be unto you: as my Father hath sent me, even so send I you. And when he had said this, he breathed on them, and said unto them, Receive ye the Holy Ghost: Who ever sins you remit, they are remitted; and who ever sins you retain, they are retained. But Thomas, one of the twelve, called Didymus, was not with them when Jesus came. The other disciples - said to him, we have seen the Lord. But he said, except I see in his hands the print of the nails, and put my finger into the nail print and thrust my hand into his side, I will not believe. After eight days again his disciples were in the room, and Thomas was with them: then Jesus came, the doors being shut, and stood in the midst, and said, Peace be unto you. Then He said to Thomas, reach out thy finger, and behold my hands; and -- thrust your hand it into my side: be not faithless, but believe. Thomas answered. My Lord and my God! Jesus said, Thomas, because you have seen me, you have believed: blessed are they that have not seen, and yet have believed. (KJV modernized for today's readers)

Appendix 4: Selected Songs.

Week one. Death and Glory.

1. All my days. SOF 1158, CH 144.
2. Beneath the Cross of Jesus. SOF 39, SV 172, MM 162, H & P 165, MHB 197, MP 55, MHB 176, MP 458, CH573.
3. How Deep the Father's Love. SOF 780, S V 180, CH 193.
4. It's your blood. SOF 257, WT 218, MP 351.
5. Man of Sorrows. SOF 385, SV183, H&P 228, MM173, CH 248
6. My Lord What Love is this? S of F 398, S V 282, W T 304, MP 476, CH 251.
7. No scenes of stately majesty. SOF 1643, WT 310.
8. Thank your for the cross. SOF 522, MP 632, WT 390.

Week two. A New family, a New faith.

1. All to Jesus I surrender, SOF1163, MP 25, MM 568.
2. At the foot of the cross, SOF 1180,
3. Come see the beauty of the Lord. SOF 74, MP 100.
4. I will build my church. SOF 264, MP 305, WT 192.
5. Jesus is Lord, SOF 290-WT 229-MP 367-MM 157-H&P 260-CH 160
6. Jesus put this song into our heart. MP 376, SOF 299, WT 239.
7. The Church's one foundation, H&P 515, MM 671, MP 640, WT 393, S of F 525, MHB 701, CH 370.
8. Thank you for saving me. SOF 1015, WT 389.

Week three. A New Hope.

1. Before the Throne. SOF 1187, WT 38, CH 296.
2. How Can I be Free from Sin? SOF 779, S V 329, WT 155.
3. I get so excited, Lord. MP 270, WT 170, SOF 209.
4. I Stand Amazed. SOF 829, SV 181, WT 183, MP 296, CH 245
5. The Servant King. SOF 120, S V 171, WT 100, MP 162.
6. There is a Fountain. MM 324, MHB 201, MP 671, CH 260
7. There's a place (Because of You) SOF 1041, WT 418.
8. Were you there? SOF 1589, H&P 181, MP 745.

[Some churches will beak the programme here for Mothering Sunday.]

Week four: The Great Cry of Dereliction.

1. All Hail the Lamb. SOF 8, SV 86, WT 6, MP 12.
2. I am Thine O Lord. SV 613, MM 561, MHB 746.
3. I Know a Place. SOF 802, SV 268, WT 173.
4. King of my Life. SV 619, MM 180, CH 247.
5. O For a thousand Tongues. SOF 412, H&P 744, MP 496, MM 15, MHB 1.
6. The Price is paid. SOF 540, SV 191, WT 407, MP 663, CH 599
7. There is a green hill far away. SOF 542, MM 172, MP 674, MHB 180, H&P 178.

8. When I Survey. SOF 596, SV 195, WT 466, H & P 180, MM 179, MHB 182, MP 755, Ch 263.

Week five: The Last Words from the cross.
1. Above all powers. SOF1151.
2. Give Me a Sight. SV 175, MM166, MP 166, CH 235.
3. It Passeth Knowledge. SV 100, H&P 526, MM 58, MHB 436, MP, 349, CH 157.
4. I Will Sing the Wondrous Story. SOF 278, SV 376, H&P 223, MM 635, MHB 380, MP 315, Ch 707.
5. Jesus Christ, (once again). SOF 865, WT 223.
6. King of Kings, Majesty. WT 252.
7. The Father's song 1321 SOF
8. Make Way.
9. We Bow down, SOF 1084, WT 442.

[Some churches may wish to break the study here for Palm Sunday.]

Week six. Easter Sunday: The Resurrection.
1. All Heaven Declares. SOF 10, SV 198, WT 7, MP 14, CH141.
2. Christ the Lord is risen, MP 76, SOF 61, MHB 204, H&P 193, MM 192, Ch 267.
3. I Cannot Tell. SOF 205, SV 159, WT 197, H&P 238, MHB 809, MP 266, CH 469.

4. In Christ alone New SOF1346 or Old CH 647.

5. In The Tomb, Christ is risen, WT212, SOF 245, MP340, CH272

6. Lord Enthroned in Heavenly Splendour. SOF 352, H&P 616, MM16, MP 431.

7. One day when Heaven, Living he loved SV162, MM 136, MP 540, CH 178.

8. Thine be the Glory, MP 551, MP 689, WT 424, H&P 212, MM191, MHB 213, CH 281.

Hymn books consulted.

Songs of fellowship, (SOF) Kingsway music 2003.
Songs of Victory (SV) Faith Mission Edinburgh, 1998.
Worship Today (WT) Spring Harvest 2000.
Hymns & Psalms, (H&P) Methodist Publishing House 1983.
Mission Praise (MP) Marshall Pickering 1995 edition.
Making Melody (MM) Assemblies of God Publishing 1983.
Methodist Hymn book. (MHB) Methodist Conference 1938.
Christian Hymns (CH) Evangelical Movement of Wales 2004.

There are a wide variety of songs chosen to fit with the subject of each week. They represent a broad selection of hymn books, old and new, the leader may of course choose their own songs. The cross is central to the Christian faith. I hope you have enjoyed the studies and have grown not just in understanding but in your love of Christ and His people.

The Lord guide and keep you always, Rev D Kevin Jones.

Appendix 5 Dressing an Easter Cross

Week 1: Activity for the whole Church on Sunday

During the Sunday service erect a bare wooden cross at the front of the church. This will remind us of our focus in the weeks ahead. If possible the cross should be head height and made form the branches of last year's Christmas tree, thus linking the birth of Christ with the death of Christ. Each week articles will be added to the cross.

Verse to be read before the cross. *Isaiah 53:4-5 'Surely he has borne our grief, and carried our sorrows: yet we esteemed him stricken, smitten of God, and afflicted. He was wounded for our transgressions; he was bruised for our iniquities: the chastisement of our peace was laid upon him; and with his stripes we are healed. KJV modernised.*

Weekly memory verse to be read out in the service.

Heb 2:8-9 'at present we do not see everything subject to him. But we see Jesus, who was made a little lower than the angels, now crowned with glory and honour because he suffered death, so that by the grace of God he might taste death for everyone.'

Week 2: Activity for the whole Church on Sunday

Take a bowl, a towel and a jug, if you wish you may wash the feet of a member of the congregation. Otherwise pour water into the bowl and place it at the foot of the cross.

Verses to read out. *John 13:4-5 + 13-15, 'Jesus rose from supper, and laid aside his garments; He took a towel, and girded himself. After that he poured water into a basin, and began to wash the disciples' feet, and to wipe them with the* *towel.* [Then He said] you *call me Master and Lord: and so I am. If I then, your Lord and Master, have washed your feet; you also ought to wash one another's feet. KJV modernised.*

Weekly memory verse to be read out in the service.

Matt 16:16-18 'Simon Peter answered, Thou art the Christ, the Son of the living God. - And Jesus answered - upon this rock I will build my church; and the gates of hell shall not prevail against it.' KJV

Week 3: Activity for the whole Church on Sunday

First take a purple robe and drape it over the cross, then write up a label and nail it to the top of the cross. If you have more than one nationality in the church, it should be in English and the two other major languages. The label should read as follows.

Verse to read. John 19:19-20 *'Pilate also wrote a title and put it on the cross; it read, "Jesus of Nazareth, the King of the Jews." Many of the Jews read this title, for the place where Jesus was crucified was near the city; and it was written in Hebrew, in Latin, and in Greek.' RSV*

Weekly memory verse to be read out in the service.

Rom 10:9-10 'if you confess with your mouth, "Jesus is Lord," and believe in your heart that God raised him from the dead, you will be saved. For it is with your heart that you believe and are justified, and it is with your mouth that you confess and are saved.'

Week 4: Activity for the whole Church on Sunday

Take a whip of cords and throw it at the base of the cross, take a crown of thorns and place it over the head of the cross.

Verse to read. *Matt 27:45-46 'Now from the sixth hour there was darkness over all the land unto the ninth hour. And about the ninth hour Jesus cried with a loud voice, saying, Eli, Eli, lama sabachthani? My God, my God, why hast thou forsaken me?' KJV*

Weekly memory verse to be read out in the service.

Gal 3:13 'Christ has redeemed us from the curse of the law, being made a curse for us: for it is written, Cursed is every one that hangeth on a tree:' KJV

Week 5: Activity for the whole Church on Sunday

Take three 6 inch nails and hammer them into the cross, one in the upright and two in the cross bar.

Verse to read. *Gal 3:13 'Christ has redeemed us from the curse of the law, having become a curse for us (for it is written, "Cursed is everyone who hangs on a tree"). NKJV*

Weekly memory verse to be read out in the service.

Col 2:13-14 'God made you alive with Christ. He forgave us all our sins, having cancelled the written code, with its regulations, that was against us and that stood opposed to us; he took it away, nailing it to the cross. NIV

Week 6: Activity for the whole Church on Sunday

(You will need to prepare sticky back hearts or put double sided tape in the cross) Make enough paper hearts for the whole congregation; they may be in many colours. Ask people to write down their sins, faults and failures, or to write their own thank you prayer. Then during a hymn or in silence take the hearts and stick them to the cross.

Reading. Acts 2:24 + 37-38. *'But God raised him from the dead, freeing him from the agony of death, because it was impossible for death to keep its hold on him. When the people heard this, they were cut to the heart and said to Peter and the other apostles, "Brothers, what shall we do?" Peter replied, "Repent and be baptised, every one of you, in the name of Jesus Christ for the forgiveness of sins and you will receive the gift of the Holy Spirit.'*

Weekly memory verse to be read out in the service.

1 Cor 15:20-21 'now is Christ risen from the dead, and become the firstfruits of them that slept. For since by man came death, by man came also the resurrection of the dead.' KJV

On the next page are the weekly memory verses which can be cut out circulated & used as bookmarks, this will help with learning the verses. They may be laminated or copied onto coloured card.

1. At present we do not see everything subject to him. But we see Jesus, who was made a little lower than the angels, now crowned with glory and honour because he suffered death, so that by the grace of God he might taste death for everyone. Heb 2:8-9 NIV

2. Simon Peter answered; Thou art the Christ, the Son of the living God. -- Jesus answered -- Upon this rock I will build my church; and the gates of hell shall not prevail against it. Matt 16:16+18 KJV.

3. That if you confess with your mouth, "Jesus is Lord," and believe in your heart that God raised him from the dead, you will be saved. For it is with your heart that you believe and are justified, and it is with your mouth that you confess and are saved. Rom 10:9-10 NIV

4. Christ hath redeemed us from the curse of the law, being made a curse for us: for it is written, Cursed is every one that hangs on a tree: Gal 3:13 KJV

5. God made you alive with Christ. He forgave us all our sins, having cancelled the written code, with its regulations, that was against us and that stood opposed to us; he took it away, nailing it to the cross. Col 2:13-14 NIV

6. Now is Christ risen from the dead, and become the firstfruits of them that slept. For since by man came death, by man came also the resurrection of the dead. 1 Cor 15:20-21 KJV

Lightning Source UK Ltd.
Milton Keynes UK
UKHW022022060119
335063UK00006B/148/P

9 780954 946210